The Abridged
Autobiography
of Benjamin Franklin

Abridged by
Daniel V. Runyon, Ph.D.

The Abridged Autobiography of Benjamin Franklin
Abridged by Daniel V. Runyon, Ph.D.

Published by Saltbox Press, 167 Burr Oak Drive, Spring Arbor, Michigan 49283

ISBN: 978 1 878559 20 3

Not intended as a scholarly resource, this abridgment is meant for enjoyable and informative reading. Please see the original text at www.gutenberg.org/ebooks/20203 for any direct quotes attributed to Franklin. The Project Gutenberg eBook text is public domain and may be used by anyone anywhere at no cost and with few restrictions.

Price: $20.00

Contents

Page **Chapter**

4   Introduction

10   **Part I: Written to his Son**

10   1. Ancestry and Early Life in Boston

20   2. Beginning Life as a Printer

31   3. Arrival in Philadelphia

40   4. First Visit to Boston

49   5. Early Friends in Philadelphia

54   6. First Visit to London

67   7. Beginning Business in Philadelphia

83   8. Business Success and First Public Service

90   **Part 2: Written after the Revolutionary War**

96   9. Plan for Attaining Moral Perfection

111   10. *Poor Richard's Almanac*

121   11. Interest in Public Affairs

129   12. Defense of the Province

137   13. Public Services and Duties

150   14. Albany Plan of Union

153   15. Quarrels with the Proprietary Governors

157   16. Braddock's Expedition

169   17. Defense of the Frontier

179   18. Scientific Experiments

183   19. Agent of Pennsylvania in London

193   Appendix A: Electrical Kite

195   Appendix B: The Way to Wealth

199   Appendix C: The Whistle

202   Appendix D: A Letter to Samuel Mather

203   Afterword: Abridging Ben

Introduction

Abridged from F. W. P., The Gilman Country School, Baltimore, September 1916.

The human aspect of the account makes Franklin's *Autobiography* different. Franklin told the story of his life to help readers by the relation of his own rise from obscurity and poverty to eminence and wealth. His accounts of these achievements are given only as a part of the story, and the vanity displayed is incidental and in keeping with the honesty of the recital.

The *Autobiography* should be an intimate friend of American young people. Here they may establish a close relationship with a foremost American, and one of the wisest men of his age.

The life of Franklin is of importance because of the part he played in securing the independence of the United States and in establishing it as a nation. Franklin shares with Washington the honors of the Revolution, and of the events leading to the birth of the new nation. To Franklin's cogent reasoning and keen satire, we owe the forcible presentation of the American case in England and France. His patience, fortitude, and practical wisdom, coupled with self-sacrificing devotion to the cause of his country, are to be admired.

Franklin is also interesting because his teachings did more than any other American to advance the material prosperity of his countrymen. It is said that his widely read maxims made Philadelphia and

4

Pennsylvania wealthy, while Poor Richard's pithy sayings, translated into many languages, have had a world-wide influence.

This graphic story of his steady rise from humble boyhood in a tallow-chandler shop, by industry, economy, and perseverance in self-improvement, to eminence, is the most remarkable of all the remarkable histories of America's self-made men.

Franklin has been aptly called "many-sided." He was eminent in science and public service, in diplomacy and in literature. He was the Edison of his day, turning his scientific discoveries to the benefit of his fellow-men. He perceived the identity of lightning and electricity and set up the lightning rod. He invented the Franklin stove and refused to patent it. He possessed a shrewdness in business and practical affairs. Carlyle called him the father of all Yankees.

He founded a fire company, helped start a hospital, and improved the cleaning and lighting of streets. He developed journalism, established the American Philosophical Society, the public library in Philadelphia, and the University of Pennsylvania. He organized a postal system for the colonies which was the basis of the present United States Post Office.

The historian Bancroft called Franklin "the greatest diplomatist of his century." He perfected the Albany Plan of Union for the colonies. He is the only statesman who signed the Declaration of Independence, the Treaty of Alliance with France, the Treaty of Peace with England, and the Constitution.

As a writer, Franklin produced his *Autobiography* and *Poor Richard's Almanac*, two works that are not surpassed by similar writing. He received honorary degrees from Harvard and Yale, from Oxford and St. Andrews, and was made a fellow of the Royal Society, which awarded him the Copley gold medal for improving natural knowledge. He was one of the eight foreign associates of the French Academy of Science.

The *Autobiography* is also valuable because of the style in which it is written. If Robert Louis Stevenson is correct that style is acquired by imitation, then writers who wish to express ideas clearly, forcibly, and interestingly cannot do better than to study Franklin's method.

Franklin's fame in the scientific world was due almost as much to his modest, simple, and sincere manner of presenting his discoveries and to the precision and clearness of the style in which he described his experiments, as to the results he was able to announce. The English chemist Sir Humphry Davy said, "A singular felicity guided all Franklin's researches, and by very small means he established very grand truths. The style and manner of his publication on electricity are almost as worthy of admiration as the doctrine it contains."

Franklin was not primarily a literary man. His aim in writing was to be helpful to his fellow-men. Writing was never an end in itself, but always a means to an end. Yet his success as a scientist, a statesman, and a diplomat was in part due to his writing ability. One admirer said, "His letters charmed all, and made his correspondence eagerly sought. His political arguments were the joy of his party and the dread of his opponents. His scientific discoveries were explained in language so simple and so clear that plow-boy and exquisite could follow his thought or his experiment to its conclusion."

The *Autobiography*, *Poor Richard*, *Father Abraham's Speech* or *The Way to Wealth*, and some of the *Bagatelles*, are as widely known abroad as any American writings. Franklin must also be classed as the first American humorist.

In his numerous parables, moral allegories, and apologues, Franklin showed John Bunyan's influence. But Franklin was essentially a journalist. In his swift, terse style, he is most like Defoe, the first great English journalist and master of the newspaper narrative. The style of both writers is marked by homely, vigorous expression, satire, burlesque, repartee.

Franklin wrote no work of the imagination. He wrote the best autobiography in existence, one of the most widely known collections of maxims, and an unsurpassed series of political and social satires.

The Story of the Autobiography

The first part of the *Autobiography* was written as a letter to his son, William Franklin, and not intended for publication. The writing is informal and personal. The second part, from 1730 on, was written with a view to publication. The entire manuscript shows little evidence of revision. In fact, the expression is so homely and natural that his grandson, William Temple Franklin, changed some phrases he thought inelegant or vulgar.

Franklin began the story of his life while on a visit to his friend, Bishop Shipley, at Twyford, in Hampshire, southern England, in 1771. He took the manuscript, completed to 1731, with him when he returned to

Philadelphia in 1775. It was left there with his other papers when he went to France the following year, and disappeared during the Revolution.

Twenty-three pages of closely written manuscript fell into the hands of Abel James, an old friend, who sent a copy to Franklin at Passy, near Paris, urging him to complete the story. Franklin took up the work at Passy in 1784. His new purpose of writing was to benefit the young reader, but the work was soon interrupted and was not resumed until 1788, when he was at home in Philadelphia. He was now old, infirm, suffering, and still engaged in public service.

Under these conditions the work progressed slowly. It finally stopped when the narrative reached the year 1757. Copies of the manuscript were sent to his friends in England and France including Monsieur Le Veillard at Paris. The first edition was published in French at Paris in 1791. It was clumsily translated and unfinished. From this faulty French edition others were printed in Germany, England, and France.

In 1867 Mr. John Bigelow purchased the original manuscript and was astonished to find that what people had been reading for years was only a garbled and incomplete version of the original. In 1868 he published the standard edition. It corrected errors in previous editions and was the first English edition to contain the short fourth part written during the last year of Franklin's life. This volume is abridged from Bigelow's editions.

In this work Franklin tells in a remarkable manner the story of a remarkable life. He displayed hard common sense and a practical knowledge of the art of living. He selected and arranged his material with the unerring instinct of the journalist for the best effects. His success is due in part to his plain, clear, vigorous English. He used homely expressions, apt illustrations, and pointed allusions.

Part 1: Writing to his Son

Chapter 1:
Ancestry and Early Youth in Boston

Dear Son: I have had pleasure in obtaining little anecdotes of my ancestors. You may remember the inquiries I made among my relations when you were with me in England, and the journey I undertook for that purpose. Imagining it may be equally agreeable to you to know the circumstances of my life, and expecting the enjoyment of a week's uninterrupted leisure in my present country retirement, I sit down to write them.

Having emerged from the poverty and obscurity in which I was born and bred, to a state of affluence and some degree of reputation in the world, which with the blessing of God so well succeeded, my posterity may like to know and imitate my life.

Given the choice, I should not object to a repetition of the same life from its beginning, only asking the advantages authors have in a second edition to correct some faults of the first. Besides correcting the faults, I might change some sinister accidents and events of it for others more favorable. However, since such a repetition is not to be expected, the next thing most like living one's life over again seems to be a recollection of that life, and to make that recollection as durable as possible by putting it down in writing.

I shall indulge the inclination so natural in old men, to talk of themselves and their own past actions; and I shall indulge it without being tiresome to others, who, through respect to age, might conceive themselves obliged to give me a hearing, since this may be read or not as anyone pleases. And, lastly, perhaps I shall a good deal gratify my own *vanity*.

Most people dislike vanity in others, but I give it fair quarter, being persuaded that it is often productive of good to the possessor. Therefore, in many cases, it would not be altogether absurd if a man were to thank God for his vanity among the other comforts of life.

And now I speak of thanking God. I desire with all humility to acknowledge that I owe the happiness of my past life to His kind providence. The complexion of my future fortune is known to Him only in whose power it is to bless to us even our afflictions.

One of my uncles once put into my hands several particulars relating to our ancestors. From these notes I learned that the family had lived in the same village, Ecton, in Northamptonshire, for three hundred years, and how much longer he knew not, on a freehold of about thirty acres, aided by the smith's business, which had continued in the family till his time, the eldest son being always bred to that business; a custom which he and my father followed as to their eldest sons.

When I searched the registers at Ecton, I found an account of their births, marriages and burials from the year 1555 only, there being no registers kept in that parish at any time preceding. By that register I perceived that I was the youngest son of the youngest son for five generations back.

My grandfather Thomas, who was born in 1598, lived at Ecton till he grew too old to follow business longer, when he went to live with his son John, a dyer at Banbury, in Oxfordshire, with whom my father served an apprenticeship. There my grandfather died and lies buried. We saw his gravestone in 1758. His eldest son Thomas lived in the house at Ecton, and left it with the land to his only child, a daughter, who, with her husband, one Fisher, of Wellingborough, sold it to Mr. Isted, now lord of the manor there. My grandfather had four sons that grew up, viz.: Thomas, John, Benjamin and Josiah. I will give you what account I can of them.

Thomas was bred a smith under his father; but, being ingenious, and encouraged in learning by an Esquire Palmer, he qualified himself for the business of scrivener. He became a considerable man in the county, was a chief mover of all public-spirited undertakings and much taken notice of and patronized by Lord Halifax. He died in 1702, January 6, just four years to a day before I was born.

John was bred a dyer, I believe of woolens, Benjamin was bred a silk dyer, serving an apprenticeship at London. He was an ingenious man. I remember him well, for when I was a boy he came over to my father in Boston, and lived in the house with us some years. He lived to a great age. His grandson, Samuel Franklin, now lives in Boston. He left behind him two quarto volumes, MS., of his own poetry, consisting of little occasional pieces addressed to his friends and relations. He had formed a short-hand of his own, which he taught me, but, never practicing it, I have now forgot it.

I was named after this uncle. He was very pious, a great attender of sermons of the best preachers, which he took down in his short-hand, and had with him many volumes of them. He was also much of a politician; too much, perhaps, for his station.

This obscure family of ours was early in the Reformation, and continued Protestants through the reign of Queen Mary, when they were sometimes in danger of trouble on account of their zeal against popery. They had an English Bible, and to conceal and secure it, it was fastened open with tapes under and within the cover of a joint-stool.

When my great-great-grandfather read to his family, he turned up the joint-stool upon his knees, turning over the leaves then under the tapes. One of the children stood at the door to give notice if he saw the apparitor coming, who was an officer of the spiritual court. In that case the stool was turned down again upon its feet, when the Bible remained concealed under it as before.

The family continued in the Church of England till about the end of Charles the Second's reign, when some of the ministers that had been outed for non-conformity, held conventicles [secret church services] in Northamptonshire. Benjamin and Josiah adhered to them, and so continued all their lives.

Josiah, my father, married young, and carried his wife with three children into New England, about 1682. The conventicles having been forbidden by law, and frequently disturbed, induced some considerable men of his acquaintance to remove to that country, and he accompanied them thither, where they expected to enjoy their mode of religion with freedom. By the same wife he had four children more born there, and by a second wife ten more, in all seventeen; of which I remember thirteen sitting at one time at his table, who all grew up to be men and women, and married

I was the youngest son, and the youngest child but two, and was born in Boston, New England. My mother, the second wife, was Abiah Folger, daughter of Peter Folger, one of the first settlers of New England, of whom honorable mention is made by Cotton Mather, in his church history of that country, entitled *Magnalia Christi Americana*, as "*a godly, learned Englishman.*"

Folger wrote sundry small occasional pieces in the home-spun verse of that time and people. One of them was printed and addressed to those in the government. It was in favor of liberty of conscience, and in behalf of the Baptists, Quakers, and others that had been under persecution. The verse ascribed the Indian wars and other distresses to that persecution, as judgments of God to punish so heinous an offense, and exhorting a repeal of uncharitable laws.

My elder brothers were all put apprentices to different trades. I was put to the grammar-school at eight years of age, my father intending to devote me, as the tithe of his sons, to the service of the Church. My early readiness in learning to read (I do not remember when I could not read), and the opinion of all his friends, that I should certainly make a good scholar, encouraged him. My uncle Benjamin, too, approved of it, and proposed to give me all his short-hand volumes of sermons, I suppose as a stock to set up with, if I would learn his character.

I continued at the grammar-school not quite one year, though in that time I had risen gradually from the middle of the class to the head of it, and then into the next class above it, in order to go with that into the third at the end of the year.

My father then took me from the grammar-school and sent me to a school for writing and arithmetic, kept by Mr. George Brownell, very successful in his profession by mild, encouraging methods. Under him I acquired fair writing, but I failed in arithmetic. At ten years old I was taken home to assist my father in his tallow-chandler and sope-boiler business. I was employed in cutting wick for the candles, filling the dipping mold and the molds for cast candles, attending the shop, and going of errands.

I disliked the trade, and had a strong inclination for the sea, but my father declared against it. However, living near the water, I was much in and about it, learnt early to swim well, and to manage boats, and when in a boat or canoe with other boys, I was commonly allowed to govern, especially in any case of difficulty.

I was generally a leader among the boys, and sometimes led them into scrapes, of which I will mention one instance, as it shows an early public spirit, though not then justly conducted.

A salt-marsh bounded part of the mill-pond, on the edge of which, at high water, we used to stand to fish for minnows. By much trampling, we had made it a quagmire. My proposal was to build a wharf there fit for us to stand upon, and I showed my comrades a large heap of stones, which were intended for a new house near the marsh, and which would very well suit our purpose.

Accordingly, in the evening, when the workmen were gone, I assembled a number of my playfellows, and working with them diligently like so many emmets, sometimes two or three to a stone, we brought them all away and built our little wharf. The next morning the workmen were surprised at missing the stones, which were found in our wharf. Inquiry was made after the removers, we were discovered and complained of, and several of us were corrected by our fathers. Though I pleaded the usefulness of the work, my father convinced me that nothing was useful which was not honest.

I think you may like to know something of his person and character. He had an excellent constitution of body, was of middle stature, but well set, and very strong. He was ingenious, could draw prettily, was skilled a little in music, and had a clear, pleasing voice, so that when he played psalm tunes on his violin and sung withal, as he sometimes did in an evening after the business of the day was over, it was extremely agreeable to hear.

He had a mechanical genius too, and was very handy in the use of other tradesmen's tools. But his great excellence lay in a sound understanding and solid judgment in prudential matters, both in private and public affairs. In the latter he was never employed, the numerous family he had to educate and the straitness of his circumstances keeping him close to his trade. But I remember well his being frequently visited by leading people, who consulted him for his opinion in affairs of the town or church, and showed a good deal of respect for his judgment and advice. He was also much consulted by private persons about their affairs when any difficulty occurred, and frequently chosen an arbitrator between contending parties.

At his table he liked to have, as often as he could, some sensible friend or neighbor to converse with, and always took care to start some ingenious or useful topic for discourse, which might tend to improve the minds of his children. By this means he turned our attention to what was good, just, and prudent in the conduct of life.

Little notice was ever taken of the victuals on the table, whether it was well or ill dressed, in or out of season, of good or bad flavor, preferable or inferior to this or that other thing. I was brought up in such a perfect inattention to those matters as to be indifferent of food set before me. This has been a convenience to me in traveling, where my companions have been unhappy for want of suitable gratification of their more delicate tastes and appetites.

My mother likewise had an excellent constitution: she suckled all her ten children. I never knew either my father or mother to have any sickness but that of which they died, he at 89, and she at 85 years of age. They lie buried together at Boston, where I placed a marble over their grave, with this inscription:

Josiah Franklin,
and
Abiah his wife,
lie here interred.
They lived lovingly together in wedlock
fifty-five years.
Without an estate, or any gainful employment,

By constant labor and industry,
with God's blessing,
They maintained a large family
comfortably,
and brought up thirteen children
and seven grandchildren
reputably.
From this instance, reader,
Be encouraged to diligence in thy calling,
And distrust not Providence.
He was a pious and prudent man;
She, a discreet and virtuous woman.
Their youngest son,
In filial regard to their memory,
Places this stone.
J. F. born 1655, died 1744, Ætat 89.
A. F. born 1667, died 1752, —— 85.

By my rambling digressions I perceive myself to be grown old. I used to write more methodically. But one does not dress for private company as for a public ball.

To return: I continued in my father's business for two years, till I was twelve years old. When my brother John left, married, and set up for himself at Rhode Island, there was all appearance that I was destined to supply his place, and become a tallow-chandler.

My dislike to the trade continuing, my father feared that if he did not find one more agreeable, I should break away and get to sea, as his son Josiah had done, to his great vexation. He therefore sometimes took me to walk with him, and see joiners, bricklayers, turners, and braziers at their work, that he might observe my inclination. It has ever since been a pleasure to me to see good workmen handle their tools; and it has been useful to me, having learnt so much by it as to be able to do little jobs myself in my house, and to construct little machines for my experiments, while the intention of making the experiment was fresh and warm in my mind.

Chapter 2:
Beginning Life as a Printer

From a child I was fond of reading, and all the money that came into my hands was laid out in books. Pleased with the *Pilgrim's Progress*, my first collection was of John Bunyan's works in separate little volumes. I afterward sold them to enable me to buy R. Burton's *Historical Collections*.

My father's library consisted chiefly of books in polemic divinity, most of which I read. I have since often regretted that, at a time when I had such a thirst for knowledge, more proper books had not fallen in my way, since it was now resolved I should not be a clergyman. Plutarch's *Lives* I read, and I still think that time spent to great advantage. There was also a book of DeFoe's called an *Essay on Projects*, and another of Dr. Mather's, *Essays to do Good*, which gave me a turn of thinking that influenced some of the principal future events of my life.

This bookish inclination at length determined my father to make me a printer, though he had already one son (James) of that profession. In 1717 my brother James returned from England with a press and letters to set up his business in Boston. I liked it much better than that of my father, but still had a hankering for the sea. To prevent such an inclination, my father was impatient to have me bound to my brother. I stood out some time, but at last was persuaded, and signed the indentures when I was yet but twelve years old.

I was to serve as an apprentice till I was twenty-one years of age, only I was to be allowed journeyman's wages during the last year. In a little time I made great proficiency in the business, and became a useful hand to my brother. I now had access to better books. An acquaintance with the apprentices of booksellers enabled me sometimes to borrow a small one, which I was careful to return soon and clean. Often I sat up in my room reading the greatest part of the night, when the book was borrowed in the evening and to be returned early in the morning.

After some time an ingenious tradesman, Mr. Matthew Adams, who had a pretty collection of books, and who frequented our printing-house, took notice of me, invited me to his library, and very kindly lent me such books as I chose to read. I now took a fancy to poetry. My brother encouraged me, and put me on composing occasional ballads. One was called *The Lighthouse Tragedy*, and contained an account of the drowning of Captain Worthilake, with his two daughters. The other was a sailor's song on the taking of Blackbeard the pirate. They were wretched stuff, in the Grub-street-ballad style, and when they were printed he sent me about the town to sell them. The first sold wonderfully, the event being recent. This flattered my vanity, but my father discouraged me by ridiculing my performances, and telling me verse-makers were generally beggars.

So I escaped being a poet, most probably a very bad one. But prose writing has been of great use to me in the course of my life, and was a principal means of my advancement.

There was another bookish lad in the town, John Collins, with whom I was intimately acquainted. We sometimes disputed, and very fond we were of argument, and very desirous of confuting one another, which is apt to become a very bad habit, making people extremely disagreeable in company. Thence, besides souring and spoiling conversation, argument produces disgust and enmity where you may have occasion for friendship. I had caught it by reading my father's books of dispute about religion. Persons of good sense, I have since observed, seldom fall into it, except lawyers, university men, and men that have been bred at Edinborough.

On the question of the propriety of educating the female sex in learning, and their abilities for study, Collins was of opinion that it was improper, and that they were naturally unequal to it. I took the contrary side, perhaps a little for dispute's sake. He was naturally more eloquent, had ready plenty of words, and bore me down more by his fluency than by the strength of his reasons.

As we parted without settling the point, I sat down to put my arguments in writing, which I sent to him. He answered, and I replied. Three or four letters had passed when my father happened to find my papers and read them. Without entering into the discussion, he took occasion to talk to me about my manner of writing; observed that, though I had the advantage of my antagonist in correct spelling and pointing (which I owed to the printing-house), I fell far short in elegance of expression, in method and in perspicuity. I saw the justice of his remarks, and thence grew more attentive to the manner of writing and determined to improve.

About this time I met with an odd volume of the *Spectator*. I bought it, read it over and over, and was much delighted. I thought the writing excellent, and wished to imitate it. With this view I took some of the papers, and, making short hints of the sentiment in each sentence, laid them by a few days, and then, without looking at the book, tried to complete the papers again, by expressing each hinted sentiment at length, and as fully as it had been expressed before, in any suitable words that should come to hand. Then I compared my *Spectator* with the original, discovered some of my faults, and corrected them.

I found I wanted a stock of words, or a readiness in recollecting and using them, which I thought I should have acquired before that time if I had gone on making verses. Writers have the continual occasion for words of the same import, but of different length, to suit the measure, or of different sound for the rhyme. Writing poetry would have laid me under a constant necessity of searching for variety, and also have tended to fix that variety in my mind, and make me master of it. Therefore I took some of the tales and turned them into verse. After a time, when I had pretty well forgotten the prose, I turned them back again. I also sometimes jumbled my collections of hints into confusion, and after some weeks endeavored to reduce them into the best order, before I began to form the full sentences and complete the paper.

This was to teach me method in the arrangement of thoughts. By comparing my work afterward with the original, I discovered many faults and amended them; but I sometimes had the pleasure of fancying that, in certain particulars of small import, I had improved the language, and this encouraged me to think I might possibly in time come to be a tolerable English writer, of which I was extremely ambitious.

My time for these exercises and for reading was at night, after work or before it began in the morning, or on Sundays, when I contrived to be in the printing-house alone, evading as much as I could the attendance on public worship which my father used to exact of me, and which indeed I still thought a duty, thought I could not, as it seemed to me, afford time to practice it.

When about 16 years of age I read Tyron's book recommending a vegetable diet. I determined to go into it. My brother, being yet unmarried, did not keep house, but boarded himself and his apprentices in another family. My refusing to eat flesh occasioned an inconvenience, and I made myself acquainted with Tryon's manner of preparing dishes, such as boiling potatoes or rice, making hasty pudding, and a few others. I then proposed to my brother that if he would give me, weekly, half the money he paid for my board, I would board myself.

He instantly agreed to it, and I found that I could save half what he paid me. This was an additional fund for buying books. But I had another advantage in it. When my brother and the rest went from the printing-house to their meals, I remained there alone. Quickly dispatching my light repast, which was often no more than a biscuit or a slice of bread, a handful of raisins or a tart from the pastry-cook's, and a glass of water, had the rest of the time till their return for study. In this I made great progress from greater clearness of head and quicker apprehension which usually attend temperance in eating and drinking.

And now it was that, being ashamed of my ignorance in figures, I took Cocker's book of Arithmetic and went through the whole by myself with great ease. I also read Seller's and Shermy's books of Navigation, and became acquainted with the geometry they contain. And I read Locke *On Human Understanding*, and the *Art of Thinking*, by Messrs. du Port Royal.

While I was intent on improving my language, I met with an English grammar (I think it was Greenwood's), at the end of which there were two little sketches of the arts of rhetoric and logic, the latter finishing with a specimen of a dispute in the Socratic method. Soon after I procured Xenophon's *Memorable Things of Socrates*, wherein there are many instances of the same method. I was charmed with it, adopted it, dropped my abrupt contradiction and positive argumentation, and put on the humble inquirer and doubter.

And being then, from reading Shaftesbury and Collins, a doubter in many points of religious doctrine, I found this method safest for myself and embarrassing to those against whom I used it. Therefore I practiced it continually, and grew very artful in drawing people, even of superior knowledge, into concessions, the consequences of which they did not foresee, entangling them in difficulties out of which they could not extricate themselves, and so obtaining victories that neither myself nor my cause always deserved.

I continued this method some few years, but gradually left it, retaining only the habit of expressing myself in terms of modest diffidence; never using, when I advanced anything that may be disputed, the words *certainly, undoubtedly,* or any others that give the air of positiveness to an opinion. Rather, I conceive or apprehend a thing to be so and so; it appears to me, or *I should think it so or so,* for such and such reasons; or *I imagine it to be so;* or *it is so, if I am not mistaken.*

This habit, I believe, has been of great advantage to me when I have had occasion to persuade men into measures that I have been promoting. And, as the chief ends of conversation are to *inform* or to be *informed,* to *please* or to *persuade,* I wish well-meaning, sensible men would not lessen their power by an assuming manner that tends to disgust, create opposition, and to defeat everyone of those purposes for which speech was given to us, to wit, giving or receiving information or pleasure.

If you would inform, a positive and dogmatic manner may provoke contradiction and prevent a candid attention. If you wish information and improvement from the knowledge of others, and yet at the same time express yourself as firmly fixed in your present opinions, modest, sensible men will probably leave you in the possession of your error. And by such a manner, you can seldom hope to recommend yourself in *pleasing* your hearers, or to persuade those whose concurrence you desire. Pope says, judiciously:

"Men should be taught as if you taught them not,
And things unknown proposed as things forgot;"

He further recommends, "To speak, though sure, with seeming diffidence." And he might have coupled with this line, "For want of modesty is want of sense."

My brother had, in 1720 or 1721, begun to print a newspaper. It was the second in America and was called the New England Courant. The only one before it was the Boston News-Letter. Some of his friends said the undertaking was not likely to succeed, one newspaper being, in their judgment, enough for America. He went on with the undertaking, however, and after having worked in composing the types and printing off the sheets, I was employed to carry the papers through the streets to the customers.

He had some ingenious men among his friends, who amused themselves by writing little pieces for this paper, which gained it credit and made it more in demand. Hearing their conversations, and their accounts of the approbation their papers were received with, I was excited to try my hand among them; but, being still a boy, and suspecting that my brother would object to printing anything of mine in his paper, I disguised my hand, and, writing an anonymous paper, put it in at night under the door of the printing-house.

My paper was found in the morning, and when his writing friends read it, commented on it in my hearing. I had the exquisite pleasure of finding it met with their approbation, and that, in their different guesses at the author, none were named but men of learning and ingenuity. I suppose now that I was lucky in my judges, and that perhaps they were not really so very good as I then esteemed them.

Encouraged by this, I wrote and conveyed in the same way to the press several more papers which were equally approved. I kept my secret till my small fund of sense for such performances was pretty well exhausted. My brother was not quite pleased, as he thought, probably with reason that it tended to make me too vain.

This might be one occasion of the differences that we began to have about this time. Though a brother, he considered himself as my master, and he expected the same services from me as he would from another, while I thought he demeaned me too much.

Our disputes were often brought before our father, and I fancy I was either generally in the right, or else a better pleader, because the judgment was generally in my favor. But my brother was passionate and had often beaten me, which I took extremely amiss; and, thinking my apprenticeship very tedious, I was continually wishing for some opportunity of shortening it.

One piece in our newspaper on some political point, which I have now forgotten, gave offense to the Assembly. He was taken up, censured, and imprisoned for a month, by the speaker's warrant, I suppose, because he would not reveal his author. I too was taken up and examined before the council; but, though I did not give them any satisfaction, they contented themselves with admonishing me, and dismissed me, considering me, perhaps, as an apprentice, who was bound to keep his master's secrets.

During my brother's confinement, which I resented a good deal, notwithstanding our private differences, I managee the paper; and I made bold to give our rulers some rubs in it, which my brother took very kindly, while others began to consider me in an unfavorable light, as a young genius that had a turn for libeling and satire. My brother's discharge was accompanied with an order of the House (a very odd one), that "*James Franklin should no longer print the paper called the New England Courant.*"

A consultation was held in our printing-house among his friends, what he should do. Some proposed to evade the order by changing the name of the paper; but my brother concluded on a better way, to let it be printed under the name of Benjamin Franklin. To avoid the censure of the Assembly, we contrived that my old indenture should be returned to me, with a full discharge on the back of it. But to secure to him the benefit of my service, I was to sign new indentures for the remainder of the term. A very flimsy scheme it was; however, the paper went on under my name for several months.

At length, a fresh difference arose between my brother and me. When he found I would leave him, he took care to prevent my getting employment in any other printing-house of the town. I then thought of going to New York, as the nearest place where there was a printer; and I was inclined to leave Boston when I reflected that I had already made myself obnoxious to the governing party, and, from the arbitrary proceedings of the Assembly in my brother's case, it was likely I might, if I stayed, soon bring myself into scrapes. And farther, my indiscreet disputations about religion began to make me pointed at with horror by good people as an infidel or atheist.

My father now sided with my brother. My friend Collins, therefore, agreed with the captain of a New

York sloop for my passage, under the notion of my being a young acquaintance of his. So I sold some of my books to raise a little money, was taken on board privately, and as we had a fair wind, in three days I found myself in New York, near 300 miles from home, a boy of but 17, without the least recommendation to, or knowledge of, any person in the place, and with very little money in my pocket.

Chapter 3:
Arrival in Philadelphia

My inclinations for the sea were by this time worn out, or I might have gratified them. But, having a trade, and supposing myself a pretty good workman, I offered my service to old Mr. William Bradford, who had been the first printer in Pennsylvania, but removed from thence upon the quarrel of George Keith. He could give me no employment, having little to do and help enough already. But, says he, "My son at Philadelphia has lately lost his principal hand, Aquilla Rose, by death; if you go thither, I believe he may employ you."

Philadelphia was a hundred miles further. I set out in a boat for Amboy, leaving my chest and things to follow me round by sea. In crossing the bay, we met with a squall that tore our rotten sails to pieces, prevented our getting into the Kill, and drove us upon Long Island. A drunken Dutchman, who was a passenger too, fell overboard. When he was sinking, I reached through the water to his shock pate, and drew him up, so that we got him in again. His ducking sobered him a little, and he went to sleep, taking first out of his pocket a book, which he desired I would dry for him. It proved to be my old favorite author, Bunyan's *Pilgrim's Progress,* in Dutch, finely printed on good paper, with copper cuts, a dress better than I had ever seen it wear in its own language. I have since found that it has been translated into most of the languages of Europe, and suppose it has been more generally read than any other book except perhaps the Bible.

Honest John was the first that I know of who mixed narration and dialogue; a method of writing very engaging to the reader, who in the most interesting parts finds himself brought into the company and present at the discourse. De Foe in his *Crusoe*, his *Moll Flanders, Religious Courtship, Family Instructor,* and other pieces, has imitated it with success; and Richardson has done the same.

When we drew near the island, we found it was at a place where there could be no landing, there being a great surf on the stony beach. So we dropped anchor and swung round toward the shore. With night coming on, we had no remedy but to wait till the wind should abate. In the meantime, the boatman and I concluded to sleep, if we could, and so crowded into the scuttle with the Dutchman, who was still wet, and the spray beating over the head of our boat, leaked through to us, so that we were soon almost as wet as he.

In this manner we lay all night, with very little rest. But, the wind abating the next day, we made a shift to reach Amboy before night, having been thirty hours on the water without victuals or any drink but a bottle of filthy rum, and the water we sailed on being salt.

In the evening I found myself very feverish, and went in to bed. Having read somewhere that cold water drank plentifully was good for a fever, I followed the prescription, sweat plentifully most of the night, my fever left me, and in the morning, crossing the ferry, I proceeded on my journey on foot, having fifty miles to

Burlington, where I was told I should find boats that would carry me the rest of the way to Philadelphia.

It rained very hard all the day. I was thoroughly soaked, and by noon a good deal tired, so I stopped at a poor inn where I stayed all night, beginning now to wish that I had never left home.

I cut so miserable a figure that I was suspected to be some runaway servant. However, I proceeded the next day, and got in the evening to an inn within eight or ten miles of Burlington, kept by one Dr. Brown. He entered into conversation with me while I took some refreshment, and, finding I had read a little, became very sociable and friendly. He must have been, an itinerant doctor, for there was no town in England, or country in Europe, of which he could not give a very particular account. He was an unbeliever and wickedly undertook, some years after, to travesty the Bible in doggerel verse, as Cotton had done Virgil. By this means he set many of the facts in a very ridiculous light, and might have hurt weak minds if his work had been published, but it never was.

At his house I lay that night, and the next morning reached Burlington, but had the mortification to find that the regular boats were gone a little before my coming, and no other expected to go before Tuesday, this being Saturday. I returned to an old woman in the town, of whom I had bought gingerbread to eat on the water, and asked her advice. She invited me to lodge at her house, and I accepted the invitation. She was very hospitable, gave me a dinner of ox-cheek with great good will, accepting only a pot of ale in return.

I thought myself fixed till Tuesday should come. However, walking in the evening by the river, a boat came by, which I found was going toward Philadelphia. They took me in, and, as there was no wind, we rowed all the way. About midnight we put toward the shore, got into a creek, landed near an old fence, with the rails of which we made a fire, the night being cold, in October, and there we remained till daylight. Then one of the company knew the place to be Cooper's Creek, a little above Philadelphia, which we saw as soon as we got out of the creek, and arrived there about eight or nine o'clock on Sunday morning, and landed at the Market-street wharf.

I have been more particular in this description of my journey, and shall be so of my first entry into that city, that you may in your mind compare such unlikely beginnings with the figure I have since made there. I was in my working dress, my best clothes being to come round by sea. I was dirty from my journey; my pockets were stuffed out with shirts and stockings, and I knew no soul nor where to look for lodging. I was fatigued with traveling, rowing, and want of rest, I was very hungry, and my whole stock of cash consisted of a Dutch dollar and about a shilling in copper. The latter I gave the people of the boat for my passage. At first they refused it on account of my rowing, but I insisted on their taking it. A man being sometimes more generous when he has but a little money than when he has plenty, perhaps through fear of being thought to have but little.

Then I walked up the street, gazing about till near the market-house I met a boy with bread. I had made many a meal on bread, and, inquiring where he got it, I went immediately to the baker's he directed me to, in Second-street, and asked for biscuit, intending such as we had in Boston. But it seems they were not made in Philadelphia. Then I asked for a three-penny loaf, and was told they had none such. So not considering or knowing the difference of money, and the greater cheapness nor the names of his bread, I bade him give me three-penny worth of any sort. He gave me three great puffy rolls. I was surprised at the quantity, but took it, and, having no room in my pockets, walked off with a roll under each arm, and eating the other.

Thus I went up Market-street as far as Fourth-street, passing by the door of Mr. Read, my future wife's father; when she, standing at the door, saw me, and thought I made, as I certainly did, a most awkward, ridiculous appearance. Then I turned and went down Chestnut-street and part of Walnut-street, eating my roll all the way, and, coming round, found myself again at Market-street wharf, near the boat I came in, to which I went for a draught of the river water. Being filled with one of my rolls, I gave the other two to a woman and her child that came down the river in the boat with us, and were waiting to go farther.

Thus refreshed, I walked again up the street, which by this time had many clean-dressed people in it, who were all walking the same way. I joined them, and thereby was led into the great meeting-house of the Quakers near the market. I sat down among them, and, after looking round awhile and hearing nothing said, being very drowsy through labor and want of rest the preceding night, I fell fast asleep, and continued so till the meeting broke up, when one was kind enough to rouse me. This was, therefore, the first house I was in, or slept in, in Philadelphia.

Walking down again toward the river, and, looking in the faces of people, I met a young Quaker man, whose countenance I liked, and, accosting him, requested he would tell me where a stranger could get lodging. We were then near the sign of the Three Mariners. "Here," says he, "is one place that entertains strangers, but it is not a reputable house; if thee wilt walk with me, I'll show thee a better." He brought me to the Crooked Billet in Water-street. Here I got a dinner, and while I was eating it, several sly questions were asked me, as it seemed to be suspected from my youth and appearance that I might be some runaway.

The next morning I made myself as tidy as I could and went to Andrew Bradford the printer. I found in the shop the old man, his father whom I had seen at New York, and who, traveling on horseback, had got to Philadelphia before me. He introduced me to his son, who received me civilly, gave me a breakfast, but told me he did not at present want a hand, being lately supplied with one. But there was another printer in town, one Keimer, who perhaps, might employ me. If not, I should be welcome to lodge at his house, and he would give me a little work to do now and then till fuller business should offer.

The old gentleman said he would go with me to the new printer; and when we found him, "Neighbor," says Bradford, "I have brought to see you a young man of your business; perhaps you may want such a one." He asked me a few questions, put a composing stick in my hand to see how I worked, and then said he would employ me soon, though he had just then nothing for me to do; and, taking old Bradford, whom he had never seen before, to be one of the town's people that had a good will for him, entered into a conversation on his present undertaking and prospects. I, who stood by and heard all, saw immediately that one of them was a crafty old sophister, and the other a mere novice. Bradford left me with Keimer, who was greatly surprised when I told him who the old man was.

Keimer's printing-house, I found, consisted of an old shattered press and one small, worn-out font of English, which he was then using himself, composing an Elegy on Aquilla Rose, an ingenious young man of excellent character, much respected in the town, clerk of the Assembly, and a pretty poet.

Keimer made verses too, but very indifferently. He could not be said to write them, for his manner was to compose them in the types directly out of his head. So there being no copy, but one pair of cases, and the Elegy likely to require all the letters, no one could help him.

I endeavored to put his press (which he had not yet used, and of which he understood nothing) into order fit to be worked with; and, promising to come and print off his Elegy as soon as he should have it ready, I returned to Bradford's, who gave me a little job to do for the present, and there I lodged and dieted. A few days after, Keimer sent for me to print off the Elegy. And now he had got another pair of cases, and a pamphlet to reprint, on which he set me to work.

These two printers I found poorly qualified for their business. Bradford had not been bred to it and was very illiterate. Keimer, though something of a scholar, was a mere compositor, knowing nothing of presswork. At this time he did not profess any particular religion, but something of all on occasion; was very ignorant of the world, and had, as I afterward found, a good deal of the knave in his composition.

He did not like my lodging at Bradford's while I worked with him. He had a house, indeed, but without furniture, so he could not lodge me; but he got me a lodging at Mr. Read's before mentioned, who was the owner of his house; and, my chest and clothes being come by this time, I made a more respectable appearance in the eyes of Miss Read than I had done when she first happened to see me eating my roll in the street.

I began now to have some acquaintance among the young people of the town, that were lovers of reading, with whom I spent my evenings very pleasantly; and gaining money by my industry and frugality, I lived very agreeably, forgetting Boston as much as I could, and not desiring that any there should know where I resided, except my friend Collins, who was in my secret, and kept it when I wrote to him.

At length, an incident happened that sent me back again much sooner than I had intended. I had a brother-in-law, Robert Holmes, master of a sloop that traded between Boston and Delaware. He being at Newcastle, forty miles below Philadelphia, heard there of me, and wrote me a letter mentioning the concern of my friends in Boston at my abrupt departure, assuring me of their good will to me, and that everything would be accommodated to my mind if I would return, to which he exhorted me very earnestly.

I wrote an answer to his letter, thanked him for his advice, but stated my reasons for quitting Boston fully and in such a light as to convince him I was not so wrong as he had apprehended.

Chapter 4:
First Visit to Boston

Sir William Keith, governor of the province, was then at Newcastle, and Captain Holmes, happening to be in company with him when my letter came to hand, spoke to him of me, and showed him the letter. The governor read it, and seemed surprised when he was told my age. He said I appeared to be a young man of promising parts, and therefore should be encouraged. The printers at Philadelphia were wretched ones; and, if I would set up there, he made no doubt I should succeed; for his part, he would procure me the public business, and do me every other service in his power.

This my brother-in-law afterward told me in Boston, but I knew as yet nothing of it. When, one day, Keimer and I being at work together near the window, we saw the governor and another gentleman (which proved to be Colonel French, of Newcastle), finely dressed, come directly across the street to our house, and heard them at the door.

Keimer ran down immediately, thinking it a visit to him; but the governor inquired for me, came up, and with a condescension and politeness I had been quite unused to, made me many compliments, desired to be acquainted with me, blamed me kindly for not having made myself known to him when I first came to the place, and would have me away with him to the tavern, where he was going with Colonel French to taste, as he said, some excellent Madeira.

I was not a little surprised, and Keimer stared like a pig poisoned. I went, however, with the governor and Colonel French to a tavern, at the corner of Third-street, and over the Madeira he proposed my setting up my business, laid before me the probabilities of success, and both he and Colonel French assured me I should have their interest and influence in procuring the public business of both governments.

On my doubting whether my father would assist me in it, Sir William said he would give me a letter to him, in which he would state the advantages, and he did not doubt of prevailing with him. So it was concluded I should return to Boston in the first vessel, with the governor's letter recommending me to my father. In the meantime the intention was to be kept a secret, and I went on working with Keimer as usual, the governor sending for me now and then to dine with him. A very great honor I thought it, and he conversed with me in the most affable, familiar, and friendly manner imaginable.

About the end of April, 1724, a little vessel offered for Boston. I took leave of Keimer as going to see my friends. The governor gave me an ample letter, saying many flattering things of me to my father, and strongly recommending the project of my setting up at Philadelphia as a thing that must make my fortune.

When we arrived at Boston, I had been absent seven months, and my friends had heard nothing of me. My unexpected appearance surprised the family; all were, however, very glad to see me, and made me welcome, except my brother. I went to see him at his printing-house. I was better dressed than ever while in his service, having a genteel new suit from head to foot, a watch, and my pockets lined with near five pounds sterling silver. He received me not very frankly, looked me all over, and turned to his work again.

The journeymen were inquisitive where I had been, what sort of a country it was, and how I liked it. I praised it much, and the happy life I led in it, expressing strongly my intention of returning to it. One of them asked what kind of money we had there. I produced a handful of silver and spread it before them, which was a show they had not been used to, paper being the money of Boston. Then I let them see my watch; and, lastly (my brother still glum and sullen), I gave them a piece of eight to drink, and took my leave.

This visit of mine offended him extremely; for, when my mother later spoke to him of a reconciliation, and of her wishes to see us on good terms together, and that we might live for the future as brothers, he said I had insulted him in such a manner before his people that he could never forget or forgive it. In this, however, he was mistaken.

My father received the governor's letter with apparent surprise, but said little of it to me for some days. Capt. Holmes returning he showed it to him, asked him if he knew Keith, and what kind of man he was; adding his opinion that he must be of small discretion to think of setting a boy up in business who wanted yet three years of being at man's estate.

Holmes said what he could in favor of the project, but my father was clear in the impropriety of it, and gave a flat denial to it. Then he wrote a civil letter to Sir William, thanking him for the patronage he had so kindly offered me, but declining to assist me, I being, in his opinion, too young to be trusted with the management of a business so important, and for which the preparation must be so expensive.

My friend Collins, a clerk in the post-office, was pleased with the account I gave him of my new country and to go there also. While I waited for my father's determination, he set out before me by land to Rhode Island, leaving his books, which were a pretty collection of mathematics and natural philosophy, to come with mine and me to New York, where he proposed to wait for me.

My father, though he did not approve Sir William's proposition, was yet pleased that I had been able to obtain so advantageous a character from a person of such note, and that I had been so industrious and careful as to equip myself so handsomely in so short a time. Therefore, seeing no prospect of an accommodation between my brother and me, he gave his consent to my returning again to Philadelphia, advised me to behave respectfully to the people there, endeavor to obtain the general esteem, and avoid lampooning and libeling, to which he thought I had too much inclination; telling me, that by steady industry and a prudent parsimony I might save enough by the time I was one-and-twenty to set me up; and that, if I came near the matter, he would help me out with the rest. This was all I could obtain, except some small gifts as tokens of his and my mother's love. Then I embarked again for New York, now with their approbation and their blessing.

The sloop putting in at Newport, Rhode Island, I visited my brother John, who had been married and settled there some years. He received me very affectionately, for he always loved me. A friend of his, one Vernon, having some money due to him in Pennsylvania, about thirty-five pounds currency, desired I would receive it for him, and keep it till I had his directions what to remit it in. Accordingly, he gave me an order. This afterwards occasioned me a good deal of uneasiness.

At Newport we took in a number of passengers for New York, among which were two young women, companions, and a grave, sensible, matronlike Quaker woman. I had shown an obliging readiness to do her some little services, which impressed her. Therefore, when she saw a daily growing familiarity between me and the two young women, which they appeared to encourage, she took me aside, and said, "Young man, I am concerned for thee, as thou hast no friend with thee, and seems not to know much of the world, or of the snares youth is exposed to. Depend upon it, those are very bad women. I can see it in all their actions, and if thee art not upon thy guard, they will draw thee into some danger. They are strangers to thee, and I advise thee, in a friendly concern for thy welfare, to have no acquaintance with them."

As I seemed at first not to think so ill of them as she did, she mentioned some things she had observed and heard that had escaped my notice, but now convinced me she was right. I thanked her for her kind advice, and promised to follow it. When we arrived at New York, they told me where they lived and invited me to come and see them.

I avoided it, and it was well I did, for the next day the captain missed a silver spoon and some other things, that had been taken out of his cabin, and, knowing that these were a couple of strumpets, he got a warrant to search their lodgings, found the stolen goods, and had the thieves punished. So, though we had escaped a sunken rock, which we scraped upon in the passage, I thought this escape of rather more importance to me.

At New York I found Collins. We had been intimate from children, and had read the same books together, but he had the advantage of more time for reading and studying, and a wonderful genius for mathematical learning, in which he far outstripped me. While I lived in Boston, most of my hours of leisure for conversation were spent with him, and he was sober and industrious, much respected for his learning by several of the clergy and other gentlemen, and seemed to promise making a good figure in life.

But, during my absence, he had acquired a habit of sotting with brandy; and I found by his own account that he had been drunk every day since his arrival at New York, and behaved very oddly. He had gamed, too, and lost his money, so that I was obliged to pay his lodgings and defray his expenses to and at Philadelphia, which proved extremely inconvenient to me.

The governor of New York, Burnet (son of Bishop Burnet), hearing from the captain that a young passenger had a great many books, desired to see me. I waited upon him accordingly, and should have taken Collins with me but that he was not sober. The gov'r. treated me with great civility, showed me his library, which was a very large one, and we had a good deal of conversation about books and authors. This was the second governor who had done me the honor to take notice of me.

We proceeded to Philadelphia. I received on the way Vernon's money, without which we could hardly have finished our journey. Collins wished to be employed in some counting-house; but, whether they discovered his dramming by his breath, or by his behavior, though he had some recommendations, he met with no success in any application, and continued lodging and boarding at the same house with me, and at my expense. Knowing I had that money of Vernon's, he was continually borrowing of me, still promising repayment as soon as he should be in business. At length he had got so much of it that I was distressed to think what I should do in case of being called on to remit it.

His drinking continued, about which we sometimes quarreled; for, when a little intoxicated, he was very fractious. Once, in a boat on the Delaware with some other young men, he refused to row in his turn. "I will be rowed home," says he.

"We will not row you," says I.

"You must, or stay all night on the water," says he.

The others said, "Let us row; what signifies it?" But, my mind being soured with his other conduct, I continued to refuse. He swore he would make me row, or throw me overboard; and coming along, stepping on the thwarts, toward me, when he came up and struck at me, I clapped my hand under his crutch, and, rising, pitched him head-foremost into the river. I knew he was a good swimmer, and so was under little concern about him.

We hardly exchanged a civil word afterward, and a West India captain, who had a commission to procure a tutor for the sons of a gentleman at Barbados, happening to meet with him, agreed to carry him thither. He left me then, promising to remit me the first money he should receive in order to discharge the debt, but I never heard of him after.

Breaking into this money of Vernon's was one of the first great errata of my life; and this affair showed that my father was not much out in his judgment when he supposed me too young to manage business of importance. But Sir William, on reading his letter, said he was too prudent. There was great difference in persons; and discretion did not always accompany years, nor was youth always without it. "And since he will not set you up," says he, "I will do it myself. Give me an inventory of the things necessary to be had from England, and I will send for them. You shall repay me when you are able; I am resolved to have a good printer here, and I am sure you must succeed."

This was spoken with such an appearance of cordiality, that I had not the least doubt of his meaning what he said. Had it been known that I depended on the governor, probably some friend that knew him better would have advised me not to rely on him, as I afterwards heard him to be liberal of promises which he never meant to keep. Yet I believed him one of the best men in the world.

I presented him an inventory of a little print-house, amounting by my computation to about one hundred pounds sterling. He liked it, but asked me if my being on the spot in England to choose the types, and see that everything was good of the kind, might not be of some advantage. "Then," says he, "when there, you may make acquaintances, and establish correspondences in the bookselling and stationery way."

I agreed that this might be advantageous. "Then," says he, "get yourself ready to go with Annis;" which was the annual ship, and the only one at that time usually passing between London and Philadelphia. But it would be some months before Annis sailed, so I continued working with Keimer, fretting about the money Collins had got from me, and in daily apprehensions of being called upon by Vernon, which, however, did not happen for some years after.

I believe I have omitted mentioning that, in my first voyage from Boston, being becalmed off Block Island, our people set about catching cod and hauled up a great many. Hitherto I had stuck to my resolution of not eating animal food, and on this occasion I considered, with my master Tryon, the taking every fish as a kind of unprovoked murder. All this seemed very reasonable. But I had formerly been a great lover of fish, and, when this came hot out of the frying-pan, it smelt admirably well. I balanced between principle and inclination, till I recollected that, when the fish were opened, I saw smaller fish taken out of their stomachs. Then thought I, "If you eat one another, I don't see why we mayn't eat you."

So I dined upon cod very heartily, and continued to eat with other people, returning only now and then to a vegetable diet. So convenient a thing is it to be a *reasonable creature*, since it enables one to find or make a reason for everything one has a mind to do.

Chapter 5:
Early Friends in Philadelphia

Keimer and I lived on a pretty familiar footing and agreed tolerably well, for he suspected nothing of my setting up. He retained his old enthusiasms and loved arguing. We therefore had many disputations. I used to work him so with my Socratic method, and cornered him so often by questions apparently so distant from any point we had in hand, and yet by degrees led to the point, and brought him into difficulties and contradictions, that at last he grew cautious and would hardly answer the most common question, without asking first, "*What do you intend to infer from that*?"

However, it gave him so high an opinion of my abilities in the confuting way, that he seriously proposed my being his colleague in setting up a new sect. He was to preach the doctrines, and I was to confound all opponents. When he came to explain the doctrines, I found several conundrums which I objected to, unless I might have my way too, and introduce some of mine.

Keimer wore his beard at full length, because somewhere in the Mosaic law it is said, "*Thou shalt not mar the corners of thy beard.*" He likewise kept the Seventh day, Sabbath. These two points were essentials with him. I disliked both but agreed to admit them on condition of his adopting the doctrine of using no animal food.

"I doubt," said he, "my constitution will bear that." I assured him it would, and that he would be the better for it. He was a glutton, and I promised myself some diversion in half starving him. He agreed to try the practice if I would keep him company. I did so, and we held it for three months. We had our victuals brought to us regularly by a woman in the neighborhood who had from me a list of forty dishes, to be prepared for us at different times, in all which there was neither fish, flesh, nor fowl.

The whim suited me from the cheapness of it, not costing us above eighteen pence sterling each per week. I have since kept several Lents most strictly without the least inconvenience, so I think there is little in the advice of making those changes by easy gradations.

I went on pleasantly, but poor Keimer suffered grievously, tired of the project, longed for the flesh-pots of Egypt, and ordered a roast pig. He invited me and two women friends to dine with him. But, the food being brought too soon to table, he could not resist the temptation and ate the whole before we came.

I had made some courtship during this time to Miss Read. I had a great respect and affection for her, and had some reason to believe she had the same for me. But, as I was about to take a long voyage, and we were both only a little above eighteen, it was thought prudent by her mother to prevent our going too far at present. Marriage, if it was to take place, would be more convenient after my return, when I should be, as I expected, set up in my business. Perhaps, too, she thought my expectations not so well founded as I imagined them to be.

My chief acquaintances at this time were Charles Osborne, Joseph Watson, and James Ralph, all lovers of reading. The two first were clerks to an eminent scrivener in the town, Charles Brockden; the other was clerk to a merchant. Watson was a pious, sensible young man of great integrity; the others rather more lax in their principles of religion, particularly Ralph, who, as well as Collins, had been unsettled by me, for which they both made me suffer. Osborne was sensible, candid, frank; sincere and affectionate to his friends, but in literary matters he was too fond of criticizing. Ralph was ingenious, genteel in his manners, and extremely eloquent. I think I never knew a prettier talker. Both of them were great admirers of poetry, and began to try their hands in little pieces. Many pleasant walks we four had together on Sundays into the woods, near Schuylkill, where we read to one another and conferred on what we read.

Ralph was inclined to pursue the study of poetry, not doubting but he might become eminent in it, and make his fortune by it, alleging that the best poets must, when they first began to write, make as many faults as he did. Osborne dissuaded him, assured him he had no genius for poetry, and advised him to think of nothing beyond the business he was bred to. I approved amusing one's self with poetry now and then, so far as to improve one's language, but no farther.

It was proposed that each of us should produce a piece of our own composing in order to improve by our mutual observations, criticisms, and corrections. As language and expression were what we had in view, we agreed that the task should be a version of the eighteenth Psalm, which describes the descent of a Deity. When the time of our meeting drew nigh, Ralph called on me first, and let me know his piece was ready. I told him I had been busy, and, having little inclination, had done nothing. He then showed me his piece for my opinion, and I much approved it, as it appeared to me to have great merit.

"Now," says he, "Osborne never will allow the least merit in anything of mine, but makes 1000 criticisms out of mere envy. He is not so jealous of you; I wish, therefore, you would take this piece, and produce it as yours; I will pretend not to have had time, and so produce nothing. We shall then see what he will say to it." It was agreed, and I immediately transcribed it, that it might appear in my own hand.

We met; Watson's performance was read; there were some beauties in it, but many defects. Osborne's was read; it was much better; Ralph did it justice; remarked some faults, but applauded the beauties. He himself had nothing to produce. I was backward; seemed desirous of being excused; had not had sufficient time to make corrections, etc.; but no excuse could be admitted; produce I must.

The poem was read and repeated; Watson and Osborne gave up the contest, and joined in applauding it. Ralph only made some criticisms, and proposed some amendments; but I defended my text. Osborne was against Ralph, and told him he was no better a critic than poet. As they two went home together, Osborne expressed himself still more strongly in favor of what he thought my production; having restrained himself before, as he said, lest I should think it flattery.

"But who would have imagined," said he, "that Franklin had been capable of such a performance; such painting, such force, such fire! He has even improved the original. In his common conversation he seems to have no choice of words; he hesitates and blunders; and yet, good God! How he writes!" When we next met, Ralph revealed the trick we had played on him, and Osborne was a little laughed at.

This transaction fixed Ralph in his resolution of becoming a poet. I did all I could to dissuade him from it, but he continued scribbling verses till *Pope* cured him. He became, however, a pretty good prose writer.

I shall just remark here, that Watson died in my arms a few years after, much lamented, being the best of our set. Osborne went to the West Indies, where he became an eminent lawyer and made money, but died young. He and I had made a serious agreement that the one who happened first to die should, if possible, make a friendly visit to the other, and acquaint him how he found things in that separate state. But he never fulfilled his promise.

Chapter 6:
First Visit to London

The governor, seeming to like my company, had me frequently to his house, and his setting me up was always mentioned as a fixed thing. I was to take letters of recommendation to his friends, besides the letter of credit to furnish me with the money for purchasing the press and types, paper, etc. For these letters I was appointed to call at different times, when they were to be ready, but a future time was still named. Thus he went on till the ship, whose departure too had been several times postponed, was on the point of sailing.

When I called to take my leave and receive the letters, his secretary, Dr. Bard, said the governor was extremely busy, but would be down at Newcastle, before the ship, and there the letters would be delivered to me.

Ralph, though married and having one child, had determined to accompany me in this voyage. It was thought he intended to establish a correspondence and obtain goods to sell on commission. But I found afterward that through some discontent with his wife's relations, he purposed to leave her on their hands, and never return again.

Having taken leave of my friends, and interchanged some promises with Miss Read, I left Philadelphia in the ship, which anchored at Newcastle. The governor was there, but when I went to his lodging, the secretary said he could not then see me, being engaged in business of the utmost importance, but should send the letters to me on board. He wished me a good voyage and a speedy return. I returned on board a little puzzled, but still not doubting.

Mr. Andrew Hamilton, a famous lawyer of Philadelphia, had taken passage in the same ship for himself and son, and with Mr. Denham, a Quaker merchant, and Messrs. Onion and Russel, masters of an iron work in Maryland, had engaged the great cabin. Ralph and I were forced to take a berth in steerage and were considered ordinary persons. But Mr. Hamilton and his son (it was James, since governor) returned from Newcastle to Philadelphia, the father being recalled to plead for a seized ship.

Just before we sailed, Colonel French came on board, showed me great respect, and I was more taken notice of. The other gentlemen then invited me, with my friend Ralph, to move into the cabin.

Understanding that Colonel French had brought on board the governor's despatches, I asked the captain for those letters that were to be under my care. He said all were put into the bag together and he could not then come at them; but, before we landed in England, I should have an opportunity to pick them out.

I was satisfied for the present, and we proceeded on our voyage. When we came into the Channel, the captain kept his word with me, and gave me an opportunity to examine the bag for the governor's letters. I found none. I picked out six or seven, that, by the handwriting, I thought might be the promised letters, especially as one of them was directed to Basket, the king's printer, and another to some stationer.

We arrived in London the 24th of December, 1724. I waited upon the stationer, who came first in my way, delivering the letter as from Governor Keith. "I don't know such a person," says he; but, opening the letter, "O! This is from Riddlesden. I have lately found him to be a complete rascal, and I will have nothing to do with him, nor receive any letters from him." So, putting the letter into my hand, he turned on his heel and left me to serve some customer.

I was surprised to find these were not the governor's letters, and after comparing circumstances, I began to doubt his sincerity. I found my friend Denham and opened the whole affair to him. He let me into Keith's character, told me there was not the least probability that he had written any letters for me, and that no one who knew him had the smallest dependence on him. He laughed at the notion of the governor's giving me a letter of credit, having, as he said, no credit to give.

On my expressing some concern about what I should do, he advised me to get some employment in the way of my business. "Among the printers here," said he, "you will improve yourself, and when you return to America, you will set up to greater advantage."

We both happened to know, as well as the stationer, that Riddlesden, the attorney, was a very knave. He had half ruined Miss Read's father by persuading him to be bound for him. By this letter it appeared there was a secret scheme on foot to the prejudice of Hamilton (supposed to be then coming over with us); and that Keith was concerned in it with Riddlesden. Denham, who was a friend of Hamilton's, thought he ought to be acquainted with it; so, when he arrived in England, which was soon after, partly from resentment and ill-will to Keith and Riddlesden, and partly from good-will to him, I waited on him, and gave him the letter. He thanked me cordially, the information being of importance to him, and from that time he became my friend, greatly to my advantage on many occasions.

But what shall we think of a governor's playing such pitiful tricks, and imposing so grossly on a poor ignorant boy! It was a habit he had acquired. He wished to please everybody, and having little to give, he gave expectations. He was otherwise an ingenious, sensible man, a pretty good writer, and a good governor for the people. Several of our best laws were of his planning and passed during his administration.

Ralph and I were inseparable companions. We took lodgings together in Little Britain at three shillings and sixpence a week—as much as we could then afford. He found some relations, but they were poor and unable to assist him. He now let me know his intentions of remaining in London, and that he never meant to return to Philadelphia. He had brought no money with him, the whole he could muster having been expended in paying his passage. I had fifteen pistoles; so he borrowed occasionally of me to subsist, while he was looking out for business.

I immediately got work at Palmer's, then a famous printing-house in Bartholomew Close, and here I continued nearly a year. I was pretty diligent, but spent with Ralph a good deal of my earnings in going to plays and other places of amusement. We had together consumed all my pistoles, and now just rubbed on from hand to mouth.

He seemed quite to forget his wife and child, and I, by degrees, my engagements with Miss Read, to whom I never wrote more than one letter, and that was to let her know I was not likely soon to return. This was another of the great errata of my life, which I should wish to correct if I were to live it over again. In fact, by our expenses, I was kept unable to pay my passage back home.

At Palmer's I was employed in composing the second edition of Wollaston's "Religion of Nature." As some of his reasoning did not appear to me well founded, I wrote a little metaphysical piece in which I made remarks on them. It was entitled "A Dissertation on Liberty and Necessity, Pleasure and Pain." I inscribed it to my friend Ralph and printed a small number. It occasioned my being more considered by Mr. Palmer as a young man of some ingenuity, though he seriously expostulated with me upon the principles of my pamphlet, which to him appeared abominable. My printing this pamphlet was another erratum.

While I lodged in Little Britain, I made an acquaintance with one Wilcox, a bookseller, whose shop was next door. He had an immense collection of second-hand books. Circulating libraries were not then in use; but we agreed that I might take, read, and return any of his books. This I esteemed a great advantage, and I made as much use of it as I could.

My pamphlet fell into the hands of one Lyons, a surgeon, author of a book entitled "The Infallibility of Human Judgment," and it occasioned an acquaintance between us. He called on me often to converse on those subjects, carried me to the Horns, a pale alehouse in Cheapside, and introduced me to Dr. Mandeville, author of the "Fable of the Bees," who had a club there, of which he was the soul, being a most facetious, entertaining companion. Lyons, too, introduced me to Dr. Pemberton, at Batson's Coffee-house, who promised to give me an opportunity of seeing Sir Isaac Newton, but this never happened.

I had brought over a few curiosities, among which the principal was a purse made of asbestos, which purifies by fire. Sir Hans Sloane heard of it, came to see me, and invited me to his house in Bloomsbury Square, where he showed me all his curiosities, and persuaded me to let him add that to the number, for which he paid me handsomely.

In our house there lodged a young milliner, who had a shop in the Cloisters. She had been genteelly bred, was sensible and lively, and of most pleasing conversation. Ralph read plays to her in the evenings, they grew intimate, she took another lodging, and he followed her. They lived together some time; but, he being still out of business, and her income not sufficient to maintain them with her child, he resolved to go from London to a country school, which he thought himself well qualified to undertake, as he wrote an excellent hand, and was a master of arithmetic and accounts.

This, however, he deemed a business below him, and confident of future better fortune, when he should be unwilling to have it known that he once was so meanly employed, he changed his name, and did me the honor to assume mine; for I soon after had a letter from him, acquainting me that he was settled in a small village where he taught reading and writing to ten or a dozen boys, at sixpence each per week, and desiring me to write to him, Mr. Franklin, schoolmaster.

I left Palmer's to work at Watts's, near Lincoln's Inn Fields, a still greater printing-house. Here I continued all the rest of my stay in London. At my first admission into this printing-house I took to working at press, imagining I felt a want of the bodily exercise I had been used to in America, where presswork is mixed with composing.

I drank only water; the other workmen, near fifty in number, were great guzzlers of beer. On occasion, I carried up and down stairs a large form of types in each hand, when others carried but one in both hands. They wondered to see, from this and several instances, that the *Water-American*, as they called me, was *stronger* than themselves, who drank *strong* beer!

We had an alehouse boy who attended always in the house to supply the workmen. My companion at the press drank every day a pint before breakfast, a pint at breakfast with his bread and cheese, a pint between breakfast and dinner, a pint at dinner, a pint in the afternoon about six o'clock, and another when he had done his day's work. I thought it a detestable custom; but it was necessary, he supposed, to drink *strong* beer, that he might be *strong* to labor.

I endeavored to convince him that the bodily strength afforded by beer could only be in proportion to the grain of the barley dissolved in the water of which it was made; that there was more flour in a pennyworth of bread; and therefore, if he would eat that with a pint of water, it would give him more strength than a quart of beer. He drank on, however, and had four or five shillings to pay out of his wages every Saturday night for that muddling liquor; an expense I was free from. And thus these poor devils keep themselves always under.

Watts, after some weeks, desired to have me in the composing-room where five shillings a week for beer was demanded of me by the compositors. I thought it an imposition and stood out two or three weeks. Accordingly, considerable little pieces of private mischief were done to me, by mixing my sorts, transposing my pages, breaking my matter, etc., and all ascribed to the chappel ghost. I soon found myself obliged to comply and pay the money, convinced of the folly of being on ill terms with those one is to live with continually.

I was now on a fair footing with them, and soon acquired considerable influence. From my example, a great part of them left their muddling breakfast of beer, bread, and cheese, finding they could with me be supplied from a neighboring house with a large porringer of hot water-gruel, sprinkled with pepper, crumbed with bread, and a bit of butter in it, for the price of the beer.

This more comfortable and cheaper breakfast kept their heads clearer. Those who continued sotting with beer all day were often out of credit at the alehouse, and used to borrow at interest from me to get beer; their *light*, as they phrased it, *being out*. I watched the pay-table on Saturday night and collected what they owed me. This, and my being esteemed a pretty good *riggite* (jocular verbal satirist), soon recommended me to the master, and my uncommon quickness at composing occasioned my being put upon all work of dispatch, which generally paid better.

My lodging in Little Britain being too remote, I found another in Duke-street, opposite the Romish Chapel. It was two pair of stairs backwards, at an Italian warehouse. A widow lady kept the house; she had a daughter, and a maid servant, and a journeyman who attended the warehouse, but lodged abroad. After sending to inquire my character at the house where I last lodged, she agreed to take me in at the same rate; cheaper, as she said, from the protection she expected in having a man in the house. She had been bred a Protestant, being a clergyman's daughter, but was converted to the Catholic religion by her husband, whose memory she much revered.

She had lived much among people of distinction and knew a thousand anecdotes of them as far back as the times of Charles the Second. She was lame in her knees with the gout and seldom stirred out of her room, so sometimes wanted company; and hers was so highly amusing to me that I was sure to spend an evening with her whenever she desired it.

Our supper was only half an anchovy each, on a very little strip of bread and butter, and half a pint of ale between us. Her conversation was the entertainment. My always keeping good hours, and giving little trouble in the family, made her unwilling to part with me, so that, when I talked of a lodging I had heard of, nearer my business, for two shillings a week, which, intent as I now was on saving money, made some difference, she bid me not think of it, for she would abate me two shillings a week for the future. So I remained with her at one shilling and sixpence as long as I stayed in London.

In a garret of her house there lived a maiden lady of seventy, in the most retired manner, of whom my landlady gave me this account: that she was a Roman Catholic, had been sent abroad when young, and lodged in a nunnery with an intent of becoming a nun; but, the country not agreeing with her, she returned to England, where, there being no nunnery, she had vowed to lead the life of a nun, as near as might be done in those circumstances.

Accordingly, she had given all her estate to charitable uses, reserving only twelve pounds a year to live on, and out of this sum she still gave a great deal in charity, living herself on water-gruel only, and using no fire but to boil it. She had lived many years in that garret, being permitted to remain there gratis by successive Catholic tenants of the house below, as they deemed it a blessing to have her there.

A priest visited her to confess her every day. "I have asked her," says my landlady, "how she, as she lived, could possibly find so much employment for a confessor?"

"Oh," said she, "it is impossible to avoid *vain thoughts*."

I was permitted once to visit her. She was cheerful and polite, and conversed pleasantly. The room was clean, but had no other furniture than a mattress, a table with a crucifix and book, a stool which she gave me to sit on, and a picture over the chimney of Saint Veronica displaying her handkerchief, with the miraculous figure of Christ's bleeding face on it. She looked pale, but was never sick; and I give it as another instance on how small an income, life and health may be supported.

At Watts's printing-house I met an ingenious young man, one Wygate, who, having wealthy relations, had been better educated than most printers. A tolerable Latinist, he spoke French and loved reading. I taught him and a friend of his to swim, and they introduced me to some gentlemen from the country who went to Chelsea by water to see the College and Don Saltero's curiosities.

In our return, at the request of the company, I stripped and leaped into the river, and swam from near Chelsea to Blackfriar's, performing on the way many feats of activity, both upon and under water, that surprised and pleased my audience.

I had from a child been delighted with this exercise, had studied and practiced all Thevenot's motions and positions, added some of my own, aiming at the graceful and easy as well as the useful. All these I took this occasion of exhibiting to the company, and was much flattered by their admiration.

Wygate, who was desirous of becoming a master, grew more and more attached to me on that account, as well as from the similarity of our studies. He at length proposed to me traveling all over Europe together, supporting ourselves everywhere by working at our business. I was once inclined to it; but, mentioning it to my good friend Mr. Denham, with whom I often spent an hour when I had leisure. He dissuaded me from it, advising me to think of returning to Pennsylvania, which he was now about to do.

I must record one trait of this good man's character. He had formerly been in business at Bristol, but failed in debt to a number of people, compounded and went to

America. There, by a close application to business as a merchant, he acquired a plentiful fortune in a few years. Returning to England in the ship with me, he invited his old creditors to an entertainment, at which he thanked them for the easy composition they had favored him with, and, when they expected nothing but the treat, every man at the first remove found under his plate a bank order for the full amount of the unpaid remainder with interest.

He now told me he was about to return to Philadelphia, and should carry over a great quantity of goods in order to open a store there. He proposed to take me over as his clerk, to keep his books, in which he would instruct me, copy his letters, and attend the store. He added, that as soon as I should be acquainted with mercantile business, he would promote me by sending me with a cargo of flour and bread, etc., to the West Indies, and procure me commissions from others which would be profitable; and, if I managed well, would establish me handsomely.

The thing pleased me; for I was grown tired of London, remembered with pleasure the happy months I had spent in Pennsylvania, and wished again to see it; therefore I immediately agreed on the terms of fifty pounds a year, Pennsylvania money—less than my present earnings, but affording a better prospect.

I now took leave of printing, as I thought, forever, and was daily employed in my new business, going about with Mr. Denham among the tradesmen to purchase various articles, and seeing them packed up, doing errands, calling upon workmen to dispatch, etc.; and, when all was on board, I had a few days' leisure.

On one of these days, I was, to my surprise, sent for by a great man I knew only by name, a Sir William Wyndham, and I waited upon him. He had heard by some means or other of my swimming from Chelsea to Blackfriars, and of my teaching Wygate and another young man to swim in a few hours. He had two sons, about to set out on their travels; he wished to have them first taught swimming, and proposed to gratify me handsomely if I would teach them.

They were not yet come to town, and my stay was uncertain, so I could not undertake it; but, from this incident, I thought it likely that, if I were to remain in England and open a swimming-school, I might get a good deal of money; and it struck me so strongly, that, had the overture been sooner made me, probably I should not so soon have returned to America. After many years, you and I had something of more importance to do with one of these sons of Sir William Wyndham, become Earl of Egremont, which I shall mention in its place.

Thus I spent about eighteen months in London; most part of the time I worked hard at my business, and spent but little upon myself except in seeing plays and in books. My friend Ralph had kept me poor; he owed me about twenty-seven pounds, which I was now never likely to receive; a great sum out of my small earnings. I loved him, notwithstanding, for he had many amiable qualities. I had by no means improved my fortune; but I had picked up some very ingenious acquaintance, whose conversation was of great advantage to me; and I had read considerably.

Chapter 7:
Beginning Business in Philadelphia

We sailed from Gravesend on the 23rd of July, 1726. For the incidents of the voyage, I refer you to my Journal, the most important part of which is the *plan* to be found in it, which I formed at sea, for regulating my future conduct in life. It is the more remarkable, as being formed when I was young, and yet being pretty faithfully adhered to quite through to old age.

We landed in Philadelphia on the 11th of October, where I found sundry alterations. Keith was no longer governor, being superseded by Major Gordon. I met him walking the streets as a common citizen. He seemed a little ashamed at seeing me, but passed without saying anything.

I should have been as much ashamed at seeing Miss Read, had not her friends, despairing with reason of my return after the receipt of my letter, persuaded her to marry Rogers, a potter. With him, however, she was never happy, and soon parted from him, refusing to cohabit with him or bear his name, it being now said that he had another wife. He was a worthless fellow, though an excellent workman, which was the temptation to her friends. He got into debt, ran away in 1727 or 1728, went to the West Indies, and died there.

Keimer had got a better house, a shop well supplied with stationery, plenty of new types, a number of hands, though none good, and seemed to have a great deal of business.

Mr. Denham took a store in Water-street, where we opened our goods. I attended the business diligently, studied accounts, and grew, in a little time, expert at selling. We lodged and boarded together; he counselled me as a father, having a sincere regard for me. I respected and loved him, and we might have gone on together very happy, but in the beginning of February, 1726/7, when I had just passed my twenty-first year, we both were taken ill. My distemper was a pleurisy, which very nearly carried me off.

I forget what his distemper was; it held him a long time, and at length carried him off. He left me a small legacy in a nuncupative will, as a token of his kindness for me, and he left me once more to the wide world; for the store was taken into the care of his executors, and my employment under him ended.

My brother-in-law, Holmes, being now at Philadelphia, advised my return to my business; and Keimer tempted me, with an offer of large wages by the year, to come and take the management of his printing-house, that he might better attend his stationer's shop.

I had heard of his bad reputation in London from his wife and her friends, and was not fond of having any more to do with him. I tried for employment as a merchant's clerk; but, not readily meeting with any, I closed again with Keimer.

I found in his house these hands: Hugh Meredith, Stephen Potts, a wild Irishman, George Webb, and David Harry. I soon perceived that his intention was to have these raw, cheap hands formed through me; and, as soon as I had instructed them, he should be able to do without me. I went on, however, very cheerfully, put his printing-house in order, which had been in great confusion, and brought his hands by degrees to mind their business and to do it better.

With these men I began to live very agreeably, for they all respected me, having found Keimer incapable of instructing them,while from me they learned something daily. We never worked on Saturday, that being Keimer's Sabbath, so I had two days for reading. My acquaintance with ingenious people in the town increased. Keimer himself treated me with great civility and apparent regard, and nothing now made me uneasy but my debt to Vernon, which I was yet unable to pay, being hitherto but a poor economist. He, however, kindly made no demand of it.

Our printing-house often wanted sorts, and there was no letter-founder in America; I had seen types cast at James's in London, but without much attention to the manner. However, I now contrived a mold, made use of the letters we had as puncheons, struck the mattrices in lead, and thus supplied in a pretty tolerable way all deficiencies. I also engraved several things on occasion, made the ink and was warehouseman.

But, however serviceable I might be, I found that my services became every day of less importance, as the other hands improved in the business. When Keimer paid my second quarter's wages, he let me know that he felt them too heavy, and thought I should make an abatement. He grew by degrees less civil, put on more of the master, frequently found fault, was captious, and seemed ready for an out breaking. I went on, nevertheless, with a good deal of patience, thinking that his encumbered circumstances were partly the cause. At length a trifle snapped our connections; for, a great noise happening near the court-house, and I put my head out of the window to see what was the matter. Keimer, being in the street, looked up and saw me, called out to me in a loud voice and angry tone to mind my business, and adding reproachful words that nettled me the more for their publicity, all the neighbors looking out on the same occasion witnessed how I was treated.

He came up immediately into the printing-house, continued the quarrel, high words passed on both sides, he gave me the quarter's warning we had stipulated, expressing a wish that he had not been obliged to so long a warning. I told him his wish was unnecessary, for I would leave him that instant; and so, taking my hat, walked out of doors, desiring Meredith, whom I saw below, to take care of some things I left, and bring them to my lodgings.

Meredith came accordingly in the evening, when we talked my affair over. He had conceived a great regard for me, and was very unwilling that I should leave the house while he remained in it. He dissuaded me from returning to my native country, which I began to think of; he reminded me that Keimer was in debt for all he possessed; that his creditors began to be uneasy; that he kept his shop miserably, sold often without profit for ready money, and often trusted without keeping accounts; that he must therefore fail, which would make a vacancy I might profit from.

I mentioned my need for money, and he then let me know that his father had a high opinion of me and was sure to advance money to set us up if I would enter into partnership with him. "My time," says he, "will be out with Keimer in the spring; by that time we may have our press and types in from London. If you like it, your skill in the business shall be set against the stock I furnish, and we will share the profits equally."

The proposal was agreeable, and I consented. His father was in town and approved of it; the more as he saw I had great influence with his son, had prevailed on him to abstain long from dram-drinking, and he hoped might break him of that wretched habit entirely, when we came to be so closely connected.

I gave an inventory to the father, who carried it to a merchant; the things were sent for, the secret was to be kept till they should arrive, and in the meantime I was to get work, if I could, at the other printing-house. But I found no vacancy there, and so remained idle a few days, when Keimer, on a prospect of being employed to print some paper money in New Jersey, which would require cuts and various types that I only could supply, and fearing Bradford might engage me and get the job from him, sent me a very civil message, that old friends should not part for a few words, and wishing me to return.

Meredith persuaded me to comply, as it would give more opportunity for his improvement under my daily instructions. So I returned, and we went on more smoothly than for some time before. The New Jersey job was obtained, I contrived a copperplate press for it, the first that had been seen in the country; I cut several ornaments and checks for the bills. We went together to Burlington, where I executed the whole to satisfaction;

and he received so large a sum for the work as to be enabled thereby to keep his head much longer above water.

At Burlington I made the acquaintance of many principal people in the province. Several of them had been appointed by the Assembly to attend the press and take care that no more bills were printed than the law directed. They were therefore, by turns, constantly with us, and generally he who attended, brought with him a friend or two for company.

My mind having been much more improved by reading than Keimer's, I suppose it was for that reason my conversation seemed to be more valued. They had me to their houses, introduced me to their friends, and showed me much civility; while he, though the master, was a little neglected. In truth, he was an odd fish; ignorant of common life, fond of rudely opposing received opinions, slovenly to extreme dirtiness, enthusiastic in some points of religion, and a little knavish withal.

We continued there near three months; and by that time I could reckon among my acquired friends, Judge Allen, Samuel Bustill, the secretary of the Province, Isaac Pearson, Joseph Cooper, and several of the Smiths, members of Assembly, and Isaac Decow, the surveyor-general. The latter was a shrewd, sagacious old man, who told me that he began for himself, when young, by wheeling clay for brick-makers, learned to write after he was of age, carried the chain for surveyors, who taught him surveying, and he had now by his industry, acquired a good estate.

Says he, "I foresee that you will soon work this man out of his business and make a fortune in Philadelphia." He had not then the least intimation of my intention to set up there or anywhere. These friends were afterwards of great use to me, as I occasionally was to some of them. They all continued their regard for me as long as they lived.

Before I enter upon my public appearance in business, it may be well to let you know the state of my mind with regard to my principles and morals, that you may see how far those influenced the future events of my life.

My parents had early given me religious impressions, and brought me through my childhood piously in the Dissenting way. But I was scarce fifteen, when, after doubting by turns of several points, as I found them disputed in the different books I read, I began to doubt of Revelation itself. Some books against Deism fell into my hands; they were said to be the substance of sermons preached at Boyle's Lectures. They wrought an effect on me quite contrary to what was intended by them; for the arguments of the Deists, which were quoted to be refuted, appeared to me much stronger than the refutations. I soon became a Deist.

My arguments perverted some others, particularly Collins and Ralph; but, each of them wronged me greatly without the least compunction, and recollecting Keith's conduct toward me (who was another free-thinker), and my own toward Vernon and Miss Read, which at times gave me great trouble, I began to suspect that this doctrine was not very useful.

My London pamphlet argued that vice and virtue were empty distinctions, no such things existing. This now appeared not so clever a performance as I once thought it; and I doubted whether some error had not insinuated itself unperceived into my argument, so as to infect all that followed, as is common in metaphysical reasoning.

I grew convinced that *truth, sincerity* and *integrity* in dealings between man and man were of the utmost importance to the felicity of life. I formed written resolutions, which still remain in my journal book, to practice them ever while I lived. I entertained an opinion that, though certain actions might not be bad *because* they were forbidden by Revelation, or good *because* Revelation commanded them, yet probably these actions might be forbidden *because* they were bad for us, or commanded *because* they were beneficial to us, in their own natures, all the circumstances of things considered.

This persuasion, with the kind hand of Providence, or some guardian angel, or accidental favorable circumstance, or all together, preserved me through this dangerous time of youth. I had therefore a tolerable character to begin the world with; I valued it properly, and determined to preserve it.

We had not been long returned to Philadelphia before the new types arrived from London. We settled with Keimer and left him by his consent before he heard of it. We found a house to hire near the market at twenty-four pounds a year, and took in Thomas Godfrey, a glazier, and his family, who were to pay a considerable part of the rent to us, and we to board with them.

We had scarce opened our letters and put our press in order before George House, an acquaintance of mine, brought a countryman to us, whom he had met in the street inquiring for a printer. This countryman's five shillings, being our first-fruits, and coming so seasonably, gave me more pleasure than any crown I have since earned; and the gratitude I felt toward House has made me often more ready than perhaps I should otherwise have been to assist young beginners.

There are croakers in every country, always boding its ruin. Such a one then lived in Philadelphia; a person of note, an elderly man, with a wise look and a very grave manner of speaking; his name was Samuel Mickle. This gentleman, a stranger to me, stopped one day at my door, and said he was sorry for me, because printing was an expensive undertaking, and the expense would be lost; for Philadelphia was a sinking place, the people already half-bankrupts, or near being so; all appearances to the contrary, such as new buildings and the rise of rents, being to his certain knowledge fallacious; for they were, in fact, among the things that would soon ruin us.

He gave me such a detail of misfortunes that he left me half melancholy. Had I known him before I engaged in this business, probably I never would have done it. This man continued to live in this decaying place, and to declaim in the same strain, refusing for many years to buy a house there, because all was going to destruction; and at last I had the pleasure of seeing him give five times as much for a house as he might have bought it for when he first began his croaking.

In the autumn of the preceding year, I had formed most of my friends into a club of mutual improvement, which was called the Junto. We met on Friday evenings. The rules that I drew up required that every member, in his turn, should produce one or more queries on any point of Morals, Politics, or Natural Philosophy, to be discussed by the company; and once in three months produce and read an essay of his own writing on any subject he pleased. Our debates were to be under the direction of a president, and to be conducted in the sincere spirit of inquiry after truth, without fondness for dispute, or desire of victory. All expressions of direct contradiction were after some time prohibited under small pecuniary penalties.

The first members were Joseph Breintnal, a copier of deeds for the scriveners, a good-natured, friendly middle-aged man, a great lover of poetry, reading all he could meet with, and writing some that was tolerable; very ingenious in many little Nicknackeries, and of sensible conversation.

Thomas Godfrey, a self-taught mathematician, great in his way, and afterward inventor of what is now called Hadley's Quadrant. But he knew little out of his way, and was not a pleasing companion; as, like most great mathematicians I have met with, he expected universal precision in everything said, or was forever denying or distinguishing upon trifles, to the disturbance of all conversation. He soon left us.

Nicholas Scull, a surveyor, afterward surveyor-general, who loved books, and sometimes made a few verses.

William Parsons, bred a shoemaker, but, loving reading, had acquired a considerable share of mathematics, which he first studied with a view to astrology, that he afterwards laughed at it. He also became surveyor-general.

William Maugridge, a joiner, a most exquisite mechanic, and a solid, sensible man. Also Hugh Meredith, Stephen Potts, and George Webb. Robert Grace was a young gentleman of some fortune, generous, lively, and witty; a lover of punning and of his friends.

And William Coleman, then a merchant's clerk, about my age, who had the coolest, clearest head, the best heart, and the exactest morals of almost any man I ever met with. He became afterwards a merchant of great note, and one of our provincial judges. Our friendship continued without interruption to his death, upwards of forty years.

The club was the best school of philosophy, morality, and politics that then existed in the province; for our queries, which were read the week preceding their discussion, put us upon reading with attention upon the several subjects, that we might speak more to the purpose. And here, too, we acquired better habits of conversation, everything being studied in our rules which might prevent our disgusting each other.

My giving this account of it here is to show something of the interest I had, for every one of these exerted themselves in recommending business to us. Breintnal procured for us from the Quakers the printing of forty sheets of their history. Upon this we worked exceedingly hard, for it was a folio, pro patria size, in pica, with long primer notes. I composed of it a sheet a day, and Meredith worked it off at press. It was often eleven at night, and sometimes later, before I had finished my distribution for the next day's work, for the little jobs sent in by our other friends now and then put us back.

So determined I was to continue doing a sheet a day of the folio, that one night, when, having imposed my forms, I thought my day's work over, one of them by accident was broken, and two pages were lost. Immediately I distributed and composed it over again before I went to bed.

This industry, visible to our neighbors, began to give us character and credit. I was told that the general opinion at the merchants' Every-night club was that our business must fail, there being already two printers in the place, Keimer and Bradford. But Dr. Baird (whom you and I saw many years after at his native place, St. Andrew's in Scotland) gave a contrary opinion: "For the industry of that Franklin," says he, "is superior to anything I ever saw of the kind; I see him still at work when I go home from club, and he is at work again before his neighbors are out of bed." This struck the rest, and we soon after had offers from one of them to supply us with stationery; but as yet we did not choose to engage in shop business.

I mention this industry even though it seems to be talking in my own praise, in order that those who shall read it may know the use of that virtue, when they see its effects in my favor throughout this relation.

George Webb, who had found a female friend that lent him the funds to purchase his time from Keimer, now came to offer himself as a journeyman to us. We could not then employ him, but I foolishly let him know as a secret that I soon intended to begin a newspaper, and might then have work for him. My hopes of success, as I told him, were founded on the fact that the only newspaper, printed by Bradford, was a paltry thing, wretchedly managed, in no way entertaining, and yet was profitable I therefore thought a good paper could scarcely fail.

I asked Webb not to mention it, but he told it to Keimer, who immediately published proposals for printing one himself, on which Webb was to be employed. I resented this, and to counteract them, I wrote several pieces of entertainment for Bradford's paper under the title of the Busy Body, which Breintnal continued some months. By this means the attention of the public was fixed on that paper, and Keimer's proposals, which we burlesqued and ridiculed, were disregarded.

Keimer began his paper, however, and, after carrying it on three quarters of a year, with at most only ninety subscribers, he offered it to me for a trifle. I took it in hand directly, and it proved in a few years extremely profitable.

Our first papers made a quite different appearance from any before in the province; a better type, and better printed. But some spirited remarks of my writing on the dispute then going on between Governor Burnet and the Massachusetts Assembly, struck the principal people, occasioned the paper and the manager of it to be much talked of, and in a few weeks brought them all to be our subscribers.

This was one of the first good effects of my having learnt a little to scribble. Another was, that the leading men, seeing a newspaper now in the hands of one who could also handle a pen, thought it convenient to oblige and encourage me. Bradford had printed an address of the House to the governor in a coarse, blundering manner; we reprinted it elegantly and correctly, and sent one to every member. They were sensible of the difference: it strengthened the hands of our friends in the House, and they voted us their printers for the year ensuing.

Among my friends in the House I must not forget Mr. Hamilton, before mentioned, who was then returned from England, and had a seat in it. He interested himself for me strongly in that instance, as he did in many others afterward, continuing his patronage till his death.

Mr. Vernon, about this time, put me in mind of the debt I owed him, but did not press me. I wrote him an ingenuous letter of acknowledgment, craved his forbearance a little longer, which he allowed me, and as soon as I was able, I paid the principal with interest, and many thanks; so that erratum was in some degree corrected.

But now another difficulty came upon me which I had never the least reason to expect. Mr. Meredith's father, who was to have paid for our printing-house, was able to advance only one hundred pounds currency, which had been paid. A hundred more was due to the merchant, who grew impatient, and sued us all. We gave bail, but saw that, if the money could not be raised in time, the suit must soon come to a judgment and execution, and our hopeful prospects must, with us, be ruined, as the press and letters must be sold for payment, perhaps at half price.

In this distress two true friends, whose kindness I have never forgotten, nor ever shall forget while I can remember anything, came to me separately, unknown to each other, and, without any application from me, offering to advance me all the money that should be necessary to enable me to take the whole business upon myself. They did not like my continuing the partnership with Meredith, who, as they said, was often seen drunk in the streets, and playing at low games in alehouses, much to our discredit. These two friends were William Coleman and Robert Grace. I told them I could not propose a separation while any prospect remained of the Meredith's fulfilling their part of our agreement, because I thought myself under great obligations to them for what they had done, and would do if they could. But, if they finally failed in their performance, and our partnership must be dissolved, I should then think myself at liberty to accept the assistance of my friends.

Thus the matter rested for some time, when I said to my partner, "Perhaps your father is dissatisfied at the part you have undertaken in this affair of ours, and is unwilling to advance for you and me what he would for you alone. If that is the case, tell me, and I will resign the whole to you, and go about my business."

"No," said he, "my father is really unable; and I am unwilling to distress him farther. I see this is a business I am not fit for. I was bred a farmer, and it was a folly in me to come to town, and put myself, at thirty years of age, an apprentice to learn a new trade. Many of our Welsh people are going to settle in North Carolina, where land is cheap. I am inclined to go with them, and follow my old employment. You may find friends to assist you. If you will take the debts of the company upon you, return to my father the hundred pounds he has advanced, pay my little personal debts, and give me thirty pounds and a new saddle, I will relinquish the partnership, and leave the whole in your hands."

I agreed to this proposal: it was drawn up in writing, signed, and sealed immediately. I gave him what he demanded, and he went soon after to Carolina, from whence he sent me next year two long letters, containing the best account that had been given of that country, the climate, the soil, husbandry, etc., for in those matters he was very judicious. I printed them in the papers, and they gave great satisfaction to the public.

As soon as he was gone, I recurred to my two friends; and because I would not give an unkind preference to either, I took half of what each had offered and I wanted of one, and half of the other, paid off the company's debts, and went on with the business in my own name, advertising that the partnership was dissolved. I think this was in or about the year 1729.

Chapter 8:
Business Success and First Public Service

About this time there was a cry among the people for more paper money, only fifteen thousand pounds being extant in the province, and that soon to be sunk. The wealthy inhabitants opposed any addition, being against all paper currency, from an apprehension that it would depreciate, as it had done in New England, to the prejudice of all creditors.

We discussed this point in our Junto, where I was on the side of an addition, being persuaded that the first small sum struck in 1723 had done much good by increasing the trade, employment, and number of inhabitants in the province, since I now saw all the old houses inhabited, and many new ones building: whereas I remembered well, that when I first walked about the streets of Philadelphia, eating my roll, I saw most of the houses in Walnut Street, between Second and Front streets, with bills on their doors, "To be let"; and many likewise in Chestnut-street and other streets, which made me then think the inhabitants of the city were deserting it one after another.

Our debates possessed me so fully of the subject, that I wrote and printed an anonymous pamphlet on it, entitled *"The Nature and Necessity of a Paper Currency."* It was well received by the common people in general; but the rich men disliked it, for it increased and strengthened the clamor for more money, and they had no writers among them able to answer it. Hence their opposition slackened and the point was carried by a majority in the House.

My friends there, who conceived I had been of some service, thought fit to reward me by employing me to print the money; a very profitable job and a great help to me. This was another advantage gained by my being able to write.

The utility of this currency became so evident as never afterward to be much disputed; so that it grew soon to fifty-five thousand pounds, and in 1739 to eighty thousand pounds, since which it arose during war to upwards of three hundred and fifty thousand pounds, trade, building, and inhabitants all the while increasing, though I now think there are limits beyond which the quantity may be hurtful.

I soon after obtained, through my friend Hamilton, the printing of the Newcastle paper money, another profitable job. He procured for me, also, the printing of the laws and votes of that government, which continued in my hands as long as I followed the business.

I now opened a little stationer's shop. I had in it blanks of all sorts, the most correct that ever appeared among us, being assisted in that by my friend Breintnal. I had also paper, parchment, chapmen's books, etc. One Whitemash, a compositor I had known in London, an excellent workman, now came to me, and worked with me constantly and diligently; and I took an apprentice, the son of Aquilla Rose.

I was in debt for the printing-house. In order to secure my credit and character as a tradesman, I took care not only to be in *reality* industrious and frugal, but to avoid all appearances to the contrary. I dressed plainly. I was seen at no places of idle diversion. I never went out a fishing or shooting; a book, indeed, sometimes debauched me from my work, but that was seldom, snug, and gave no scandal; and, to show that I was not above my business, I sometimes brought home the paper I purchased at the stores through the streets on a wheelbarrow.

Thus being esteemed an industrious, thriving young man, and paying duly for what I bought, the merchants who imported stationery solicited my custom. Others proposed supplying me with books, and I went on swimmingly. In the meantime, Keimer's credit and business declining daily and he was at last forced to sell his printing-house to satisfy his creditors. He went to Barbados, and there lived some years in very poor circumstances.

His apprentice, David Harry, whom I had instructed while I worked with him, set up in his place at Philadelphia, having bought his materials. I was at first apprehensive of a powerful rival in Harry, as his friends were very able and had a good deal of interest. I therefore proposed a partnership to him, which he, fortunately for me, rejected with scorn. He was very proud, dressed like a gentleman, lived expensively, took much diversion and pleasure abroad, ran in debt, and neglected his business. Upon which, all business left him; and, finding nothing to do, he followed Keimer to Barbados, taking the printing-house with him.

There this apprentice employed his former master as a journeyman; they quarreled often. Harry went continually behindhand, and at length was forced to sell his types and return to his country work in Pennsylvania.

The person that bought them employed Keimer to use them, but in a few years he died.

There remained now no competitor with me at Philadelphia but the old one, Bradford; who was rich and easy, did a little printing now and then by straggling hands, but was not very anxious about the business. However, as he kept the post-office, it was imagined he had better opportunities of obtaining news; his paper was thought a better distributer of advertisements than mine, and therefore had many more, which was a profitable thing to him.

Though I did indeed receive and send papers by the post, yet the public opinion was otherwise, for what I did send was by bribing the riders, who took them privately, Bradford being unkind enough to forbid it, which occasioned some resentment on my part. I thought so meanly of him for it, that when I afterward came into his situation, I took care never to imitate it.

I had hitherto continued to board with Godfrey, who lived in part of my house with his wife and children and had one side of the shop for his glazier's business, though he worked little, being always absorbed in his mathematics. Mrs. Godfrey projected a match for me with a relation's daughter, took opportunities of bringing us often together, till a serious courtship on my part ensued, the girl being in herself very deserving.

The old folks encouraged me by continual invitations to supper, and by leaving us together, till at length it was time to explain. Mrs. Godfrey managed our little treaty. I let her know that I expected as much money with their daughter as would pay off my remaining debt for the printing-house, which I believe was not then above a hundred pounds.

She brought me word they had no such sum to spare. I said they might mortgage their house in the loan-office. The answer to this, after some days, was that they did not approve the match. On inquiry of Bradford, they had been informed the printing business was not a profitable one; the types would soon be worn out, and more wanted; that Keimer and Harry had failed one after the other, and I should probably soon follow them.

Whether this was a real change of sentiment or only artifice, I know not; but I suspected the latter, resented it, and went no more. Mrs. Godfrey brought me some more favorable accounts of their disposition, and would have drawn me on again, but I declared my resolution to have nothing more to do with that family. This was resented by the Godfreys and they removed, leaving me the whole house, and I resolved to take no more inmates.

But this affair turned my thoughts to marriage. I looked around me and made overtures in other places but soon found that, the business of a printer being generally thought a poor one, I was not to expect money with a wife, unless with such a one as I should not otherwise think agreeable.

A friendly correspondence had continued between me and Mrs. Read's family, who all had a regard for me from the time of my first lodging in their house. I was often invited there and consulted in their affairs, wherein I sometimes was of service. I pitied poor Miss Read's unfortunate situation, who was generally dejected, seldom cheerful, and avoided company. I considered my giddiness and inconstancy when in London as in a great degree the cause of her unhappiness, though the mother was good enough to think the fault more her own than mine, as she had prevented our marrying before I went thither, and persuaded the other match in my absence.

Our mutual affection was revived, but there were now great objections to our union. The match was indeed looked upon as invalid, a preceding wife being said to be living in England; but this could not easily be proved, because of the distance. And though there was a report of his death, it was not certain. Then, though it should be true, he had left many debts, which his successor might be called upon to pay.

We ventured, however, over all these difficulties, and I took her to wife, September 1st, 1730. None of the inconveniences happened that we had apprehended; she proved a good and faithful helpmate, assisted me much by attending the shop. We throve together, and have ever mutually endeavored to make each other happy. Thus I corrected that great *erratum* as well as I could.

About this time, our club made a proposition that, since our books were often referred to in our discussions, it might be convenient to have them altogether where we met. By clubbing our books to a common library, we should each have the advantage of using the books of all the other members, which would be nearly as beneficial as if each owned the whole.

It was liked and agreed to, and we filled one end of the room with books. The number was not so great as we expected; and though they had been of great use, yet some inconveniences occurring for want of due care of them. The collection was separated after about a year, and each took his books home again.

And now I began my first project of a public nature, that for a subscription library. I drew up the proposals, got them put into form by our great scrivener, Brockden, and, by the help of my friends in the Junto, procured fifty subscribers of forty shillings each to begin with, and ten shillings a year for fifty years. We afterward obtained a charter, the company being increased to one hundred: this was the mother of all the North American subscription libraries, now so numerous.

These libraries have improved the general conversation of the Americans, made the common tradesmen and farmers as intelligent as most gentlemen from other countries, and perhaps have contributed to the stand so generally made throughout the colonies in defense of their privileges.

Part 2: Written after the Revolutionary War

What follows was written many years later; the affairs of the Revolution occasioned the interruption.

Continuation of the Account of my Life, begun at Passy, near Paris, 1784.

At the time I established myself in Pennsylvania, there was not a good bookseller's shop in any of the colonies south of Boston. In New York and Philadelphia the printers were stationers that sold only paper, almanacs, ballads, and a few common school-books. Those who loved reading were obliged to send for their books from England; the members of the Junto had each a few.

We had left the alehouse, where we first met, and hired a room to hold our club in. I proposed that we should all bring our books to that room for the common benefit. Finding the advantage of this little collection, I proposed to render the benefit from books more common by starting a public subscription library. I drew a sketch of the plan and rules that would be necessary, and got a skilful conveyancer, Mr. Charles Brockden, to put the whole in form of articles of agreement to be subscribed, by which each subscriber engaged to pay a certain sum down for the first purchase of books, and an annual contribution for increasing them.

So few were the readers at that time in Philadelphia, and the majority of us so poor, that I was not able to find more than fifty persons, mostly young tradesmen, willing to pay forty shillings each, and ten shillings per annum. On this little fund we began.

The books were imported and the library was opened one day a week for lending to subscribers on their promissory notes to pay double the value if not duly returned. The institution was soon imitated by other towns and in other provinces. The libraries were augmented by donations. Reading became fashionable, and our people, having no public amusements to divert their attention from study, became better acquainted with books, and in a few years were observed by strangers to be better instructed and more intelligent than people of the same rank in other countries.

The objections and reluctances I met with in soliciting the subscriptions made me soon feel the impropriety of presenting one's self as the proposer of any useful project that might be supposed to raise one's reputation above that of one's neighbors, when one has need of their assistance to accomplish that project.

I therefore put myself out of sight, and stated it as a scheme of a *number of friends*, who had requested me to go about and propose it to such as they thought lovers of reading. In this way my affair went on more smoothly, and I ever after practiced it on such occasions. From my frequent successes, I can heartily recommend this approach. The present little sacrifice of your vanity will afterward be amply repaid. If it remains a while uncertain to whom the merit belongs, someone more vain than yourself will be encouraged to claim it, and then even envy will be disposed to do you justice by plucking those assumed feathers, and restoring them to their right owner.

This library afforded me the means of improvement by constant study, for which I set apart an hour or two each day, and thus repaired in some degree the loss of the education my father once intended for me. Reading was the only amusement I allowed myself. I spent no time in taverns, games, or frolics of any kind, and my industry in my business continued as indefatigable as it was necessary.

I was in debt for my printing-house, I had a young family coming on to be educated, and I had to contend with two printers who were established in the place before me. My circumstances, however, grew daily easier. My original habits of frugality continuing, and my father having, among his instructions to me when a boy, frequently repeated a proverb of Solomon, "Seest thou a man diligent in his calling, he shall stand before kings, he shall not stand before mean men," I from then on considered industry as a means of obtaining wealth and distinction. I did not think that I should ever literally *stand before kings*, which, however, has since happened; for I have stood before *five*, and even had the honor of sitting down to dinner with the King of Denmark.

We have an English proverb that says, "*He that would thrive, must ask his wife*." It was lucky for me that I had one as much disposed to industry and frugality as myself. She assisted me cheerfully in my business, folding and stitching pamphlets, tending shop, purchasing old linen rags for the paper-makers, etc. We kept no idle servants, our table was plain and simple, our furniture the cheapest. For instance, my breakfast was for a long time break and milk (no tea), and I ate it out of a two penny earthen porringer, with a pewter spoon.

But mark how luxury will enter families in spite of principle: being called one morning to breakfast, I found it in a China bowl, with a silver spoon! They had been bought for me without my knowledge by my wife, and had cost her the enormous sum of three-and-twenty shillings, for which she had no other excuse or apology to make, but that she thought *her* husband deserved a silver spoon and China bowl as well as any of his neighbors. This was the first appearance of plate and China in our house, which afterward, in a course of years, as our wealth increased, augmented gradually to several hundred pounds in value.

I had been religiously educated as a Presbyterian; and though some of the dogmas of that persuasion appeared to me unintelligible, others doubtful, and I early absented myself from the public assemblies of the sect, Sunday being my studying day, I never was without some religious principles. I never doubted, for instance, the existence of the Deity; that he made the world, and governed it by his Providence; that the most acceptable service of God was the doing good to man; that our souls are immortal; and that all crime will be punished, and virtue rewarded, either here or hereafter.

These I esteemed the essentials of every religion; and, being found in all the religions we had in our country, I respected them all, though with different degrees of respect. This respect to all, with an opinion that the worst had some good effects, induced me to avoid all discourse that might tend to lessen the good opinion another might have of his own religion. As our province increased in people and new places of worship were continually wanted, and generally erected by voluntary contribution, my mite for such purpose, whatever might be the sect, was never refused.

Though I seldom attended any public worship, I had still an opinion of its propriety, and of its utility when rightly conducted, and I regularly paid my annual subscription for the support of the only Presbyterian minister or meeting we had in Philadelphia. He used to visit me sometimes as a friend, and admonished me to attend his administrations, and I was now and then prevailed on to do so, once for five Sundays successively.

Had he been in my opinion a good preacher, perhaps I might have continued, notwithstanding the occasion I had for the Sunday's leisure in my course of study. But his discourses were chiefly either polemic arguments, or explications of the peculiar doctrines of our sect, and were all to me very dry, uninteresting, and unedifying, since not a single moral principle was inculcated or enforced, their aim seeming to be rather to make us Presbyterians than good citizens.

At length he took for his text that verse of the fourth chapter of Philippians, "*Finally, brethren, whatsoever things are true, honest, just, pure, lovely, or of good report, if there be any virtue, or any praise, think on these things.*" I imagined, in a sermon on such a text, we could not miss of having some morality. But he confined himself to five points only, as meant by the apostle, viz.: 1. Keeping holy the Sabbath day. 2. Being diligent in reading the holy Scriptures. 3. Attending duly the public worship. 4. Partaking of the Sacrament. 5. Paying due respect to God's ministers.

These might be all good things, but as they were not the kind of good things that I expected from that text, I despaired of ever meeting with them from any other, was disgusted, and attended his preaching no more. I had some years before composed a little Liturgy, or form of prayer, for my own private use. I returned to the use of this and went no more to the public assemblies. My conduct might be blamable, but I leave it, without attempting further to excuse it, my present purpose being to relate facts and not to make apologies for them.

Chapter 9:
Plan for Attaining Moral Perfection

About this time I conceived the bold and arduous project of arriving at moral perfection. I wished to live without committing any fault at any time; I would conquer all that either natural inclination, custom, or company might lead me into. As I knew, or thought I knew, what was right and wrong, I did not see why I might not always do the one and avoid the other.

But I soon found I had undertaken a task of more difficulty than I had imagined. While my care was employed in guarding against one fault, I was often surprised by another. Habit took the advantage of inattention, and inclination was sometimes too strong for reason.

I concluded that the mere speculative conviction that it was our interest to be completely virtuous was not sufficient to prevent our slipping; and that the contrary habits must be broken, and good ones acquired and established, before we can have any dependence on a steady, uniform rectitude of conduct. For this purpose I therefore contrived the following method.

In the various enumerations of the moral virtues I had met with in my reading, I found the writers included more or fewer ideas under the same name. Temperance, for example, was by some confined to eating and drinking, while by others it was extended to mean moderating every other pleasure, appetite, inclination, or passion, bodily or mental, even to our avarice and ambition.

I proposed to myself, for the sake of clearness, to use more names with fewer ideas annexed to each, than few names with more ideas. I included under thirteen names of virtues all that at that time occurred to me as necessary or desirable, and annexed to each a short precept which fully expressed the extent I gave to its meaning. These virtues, with their precepts, were:

1. **Temperance:** Eat not to dullness; drink not to elevation.

2. **Silence:** Speak not but what may benefit others or yourself; avoid trifling conversation.

3. **Order:** Let all your things have their places; let each part of your business have its time.

4. **Resolution**: Resolve to perform what you ought; perform without fail what you resolve.

5. **Frugality**: Make no expense but to do good to others or yourself; *i. e.*, waste nothing.

6. **Industry**: Lose no time; be always employed in something useful; cut off all unnecessary actions.

7. **Sincerity**: Use no hurtful deceit; think innocently and justly; and, if you speak, speak accordingly.

8. **Justice**: Wrong none by doing injuries, or omitting the benefits that are your duty.

9. **Moderation**: Avoid extremes; forbear resenting injuries so much as you think they deserve.

10. **Cleanliness**: Tolerate no uncleanliness in body, cloths, or habitation.

11. **Tranquility**: Be not disturbed at trifles, or at accidents common or unavoidable.

12. **Chastity**.

13. **Humility**: Imitate Jesus and Socrates.

My intention being to acquire the *habitude* of all these virtues, I judged it would be well not to distract my attention by attempting the whole at once, but to fix it on one of them at a time. When I should be master of that, then to proceed to another, and so on, till I should have gone through the thirteen.

As the previous acquisition of some might facilitate the acquisition of certain others, I arranged them with that view, as they stand above. Temperance first, as it tends to procure that coolness and clearness of head which is so necessary where constant vigilance was to be kept up, and guard maintained against the unremitting attraction of ancient habits, and the force of perpetual temptations. This being acquired and established, Silence would be easier.

My desire was to gain knowledge at the same time that I improved in virtue. Considering that in conversation it was obtained rather by the use of the ears than of the tongue, and therefore wishing to break my habit of prattling, punning, and joking, which only made me acceptable to trifling company, I gave *Silence* the second place.

This and the next, *Order*, I expected would allow me more time for attending to my project and my studies. *Resolution*, once become habitual, would keep me firm in my endeavors to obtain all the subsequent virtues. *Frugality* and Industry would free me from my remaining debt, and producing affluence and independence, which would make more easy the practice of Sincerity and Justice, etc., etc.

Conceiving then, that daily examination would be necessary, I contrived the following method for conducting that examination. I made a little book in which I allotted a page for each of the virtues. I ruled each page with red ink, so as to have seven columns, one for each day of the week, marking each column with a letter for the day. I crossed these columns with thirteen red lines, marking the beginning of each line with the first letter of one of the virtues, on which line, and in its proper column, I might mark, by a little black spot, every fault I found upon examination to have been committed respecting that virtue upon that day.

Sample form of the pages:

TEMPERANCE						
EAT NOT TO DULLNESS DRINK NOT TO ELEVATION						
	S	]		\		S.
	*	:		)		
(	*	:				*
]						
]		:				

I determined to give a week's strict attention to each of the virtues successively. Thus, in the first week, my great guard was to avoid every the least offense against *Temperance*, leaving the other virtues to their ordinary chance, only marking every evening the faults of the day. Thus, if in the first week I could keep my first line, marked T, clear of spots, I supposed the habit of that virtue so much strengthened, and its opposite weakened, that I might venture extending my attention to include the next, and for the following week keep both lines clear of spots.

Proceeding thus to the last, I could go through a course complete in thirteen weeks, and four courses in a year. Like him who, having a garden to weed, does not attempt to eradicate all the bad herbs at once, but works on one bed at a time, and, having accomplished the first, proceeds to a second, so I should have the encouraging pleasure of seeing on my pages the progress I made in virtue, by clearing successively my lines of their spots, till in the end I should be happy in viewing a clean book, after thirteen weeks of daily examination.

My little book had for its motto these lines from Addison's *Cato*:

"Here will I hold. If there's a power above us
(And that there is, all nature cries aloud
Through all her works), He must delight in virtue;
And that which he delights in must be happy."

Another from the Proverbs of Solomon, speaking of wisdom or virtue: "Length of days is in her right hand, and in her left hand riches and honor. Her ways are ways of pleasantness, and all her paths are peace." iii. 16, 17.

And conceiving God to be the fountain of wisdom, I thought it right and necessary to solicit his assistance for obtaining it. To this end I formed the following little prayer, which was prefixed to my tables of examination, for daily use:

"*O powerful Goodness! bountiful Father! merciful Guide! Increase in me that wisdom which discovers my truest interest. Strengthen my resolutions to perform what that wisdom dictates. Accept my kind offices to thy other children as the only return in my power for thy continual favors to me.*"

I used also sometimes a little prayer which I took from Thomson's Poems, viz.:

"Father of light and life, thou Good Supreme!
O teach me what is good; teach me Thyself!
Save me from folly, vanity, and vice,
From every low pursuit; and fill my soul
With knowledge, conscious peace, and virtue pure;
Sacred, substantial, never-fading bliss!"

The precept of *Order* requiring that *every part of my business should have its allotted time*, one page in my little book contained a scheme of employment for the twenty-four hours of a natural day.

I entered upon the execution of this plan for self-examination, and continued it for some time. I was surprised to find myself so much fuller of faults than I had imagined, but I had the satisfaction of seeing them diminish.

To avoid the trouble of renewing now and then my little book, which, by scraping out the marks on the paper of old faults to make room for new ones in a new course, became full of holes, I transferred my tables and precepts to the ivory leaves of a memorandum book. Here the lines were drawn with red ink, and on those lines I marked my faults with a black-lead pencil, which marks I could easily erase. After a while I went through one course only in a year, and afterward only one in several years, till at length I omitted them entirely, being employed in voyages and business abroad, with a multiplicity of affairs that interfered. But I always carried my little book with me.

My scheme of Order gave me the most trouble, and I found that, though it might be practicable where a man's business was such as to leave him the disposition of his time, that of a journeyman printer, for instance, it was not possible to be exactly observed by a master, who must mix with the world, and often receive people of business at their own hours.

Order, too, with regard to places for things, papers, etc., I found extremely difficult to acquire. I had not been early accustomed to it. This article, therefore, cost me much painful attention, and my faults in it vexed me so much, and I made so little progress and had such frequent relapses that I was almost ready to give up the attempt.

I would be content with a faulty character in that respect, like the man who, in buying an ax of a smith, desired to have the whole of its surface as bright as the edge. The smith consented to grind it bright for him if he would turn the wheel. He turned, while the smith pressed the broad face of the ax hard and heavily on the stone, which made the turning of it very fatiguing. The man came every now and then from the wheel to see how the work went on, and at length would take his ax as it was, without farther grinding.

"No," said the smith, "turn on, turn on; we shall have it bright by-and-by; as yet, it is only speckled."

"Yes," says the man, "*but I think I like a speckled ax best*." This may be the case with many who have, for lack of some such means as I employed, found the difficulty of obtaining good habits and breaking bad ones, have given up the struggle and concluded that "*a speckled ax was best.*"

Something that pretended to be reason every now and then suggested to me that such extreme nicety as I exacted of myself might be a kind of foppery in morals, which, if it were known, would make me ridiculous. A perfect character might be envied and hated, and a benevolent man should allow a few faults in himself to keep his friends in countenance.

In truth, I found myself incorrigible with respect to Order. And now I am grown old, and my memory bad, I feel the want of it. But, on the whole, though I never arrived at the perfection I had been so ambitious of obtaining, yet I was, by the endeavor, a better and a happier man than I otherwise should have been if I had not attempted it, just as those who aim at perfect writing by imitating the engraved copies, though they never reach the wished-for excellence, their hand is mended by the endeavor and is tolerable while it continues fair and legible.

My posterity should be informed that to this little artifice, with the blessing of God, their ancestor owed the constant felicity of his life, down to his 79th year, in which this is written. To Temperance he ascribes his long-continued health, and what is still left to him of a good constitution. To Industry and Frugality he ascribes the early easiness of his circumstances and acquisition of his fortune, with all that knowledge that enabled him to be a useful citizen, and obtained for him some degree of reputation among the learned. To Sincerity and Justice he ascribes the confidence of his country and the honorable employs it conferred upon him. And to the joint influence of the whole mass of the virtues, even in the imperfect state he was able to acquire them, he ascribes his evenness of temper and cheerfulness in conversation which makes his company still sought after. I hope, therefore, that some of my descendants may follow the example and reap the benefit.

It will be remarked that, though my scheme was not wholly without religion, there was in it no mark of any of the distinguishing tenets of any particular sect. I purposely avoided them, being persuaded that the utility and excellency of my method might be serviceable to people in all religions.

Intending some time or other to publish it, I would not have anything in it that should prejudice anyone, of any sect, against it. I purposed writing a little comment on each virtue, in which I would have shown the advantages of possessing it, and the mischiefs attending its opposite vice. I would have called my book *The Art of Virtue*, because it would have shown the means and manner of obtaining virtue, which would have distinguished it from the mere exhortation to be good, that does not instruct and indicate the means.

My intention of writing and publishing this book was never fulfilled. I did, from time to time, put down short hints of the sentiments and reasons to be used in it, some of which I still have, but the necessary close attention to private business in the earlier part of my life, and public business since, have caused me to postpone it. The book idea is connected in my mind with *a great and extensive project* that would require the whole man to execute, and it has remained unfinished.

In this piece it was my design to explain that vicious actions are not hurtful because they are forbidden, but forbidden because they are hurtful.

Considering the nature of man, it is in everyone's interest to be virtuous who wishes to be happy even in this world. And I should have endeavored to convince young persons that no qualities are so likely to make a poor man's fortune as those of probity and integrity.

My list of virtues contained at first but twelve, but a Quaker friend kindly informed me that I was generally thought proud, and that my pride showed itself frequently in conversation. I was not content with being in the right when discussing any point, but was overbearing, and rather insolent, of which he convinced me by mentioning several instances. I therefore determined to cure myself, if I could, of this vice or folly, and I added *Humility* to my list, giving an extensive meaning to the word.

I cannot boast of much success in acquiring the *reality* of this virtue, but I had a good deal with regard to the *appearance* of it. I made it a rule to forbear all direct contradiction to the sentiments of others, and all positive assertion of my own. I even forbid myself, agreeably to the old laws of our Junto, the use of every word or expression in the language that imported a fixed opinion, such as *certainly, undoubtedly*, etc., and I adopted, instead of them, *I conceive, I apprehend*, or *I imagine* a thing to be so or so; or it *so appears to me at present*.

When another asserted something that I thought an error, I denied myself the pleasure of contradicting him abruptly, and of showing immediately some absurdity in his proposition. And in answering I began by observing that in certain cases his opinion would be right, but in the present case there *appeared* or *seemed* to me some difference, etc.

I soon found the advantage of this change in my manner. The conversations I engaged in went on more pleasantly. The modest way in which I proposed my opinions procured them a readier reception and less contradiction. I had less mortification when I was found to be in the wrong, and I more easily prevailed with others to give up their mistakes and join with me when I happened to be in the right.

This mode, which I at first put on with some violence to natural inclination, became at length so easy, and so habitual to me, that for these fifty years past no one has ever heard a dogmatic expression escape me. To this habit (after my character of integrity) I owe much influence in public councils, for I was a bad speaker, never eloquent, subject to much hesitation in my choice of words, hardly correct in language, and yet I generally carried my points.

None of our natural passions is so hard to subdue as *pride*. Disguise it, struggle with it, beat it down, stifle it, mortify it as much as one pleases, it is still alive, and will every now and then peep out and show itself. You will see it, perhaps, often in this history. Even if I could conceive that I had completely overcome it, I should probably be proud of my humility.

[Thus far written at Passy, 1784. *"I am now about to write at home, August, 1788, but cannot have the help expected from my papers, many of them being lost in the war. I have, however, found the following."*]

Having mentioned *a great and extensive project* which I had conceived, it seems proper that some account should be given of that project and its object. Its first rise in my mind appears in some *Observations* on my reading history, in Library, May 19th, 1731.

"That the great affairs of the world, the wars, revolutions, etc., are carried on and effected by parties.

"That the view of these parties is their present general interest, or what they take to be such.

"That the different views of these different parties occasion all confusion.

"That while a party is carrying on a general design, each man has his particular private interest in view.

"That as soon as a party has gained its general point, each member becomes intent upon his particular interest; which, thwarting others, breaks that party into divisions, and occasions more confusion.

"That few in public affairs act from a mere view of the good of their country, whatever they may pretend; and, though their actings bring real good to their country, yet men primarily considered that their own and their country's interest was united, and did not act from a principle of benevolence.

"That fewer still, in public affairs, act with a view to the good of mankind.

"There seems to me at present to be great occasion for raising a United Party for Virtue, by forming the virtuous and good men of all nations into a regular body, to be governed by suitable good and wise rules, which good and wise men may probably be more unanimous in their obedience to, than common people are to common laws. I at present think that whoever attempts this aright, and is well qualified, cannot fail of pleasing God, and of meeting with success."

Revolving this project in my mind as to be undertaken hereafter, I put down on pieces of paper such thoughts as occurred to me respecting it. Most of these are lost, but I find one purporting to be the substance of an intended creed, containing, as I thought, the essentials of every known religion, and being free of everything that might shock the professors of any religion. It is expressed in these words:

"That there is one God, who made all things.

"That he governs the world by his providence.

"That he ought to be worshiped by adoration, prayer, and thanksgiving.

"But that the most acceptable service of God is doing good to man.

"That the soul is immortal.

"And that God will certainly reward virtue and punish vice, either here or hereafter."

My ideas were that the sect should be begun and spread at first among young and single men only, that each person to be initiated should not only declare his assent to such creed, but should have exercised himself with the thirteen weeks' examination and practice of the virtues, as in the before-mentioned model; that the existence of such a society should be kept a secret till it was well established in order to prevent solicitations for the admission of improper persons.

The members should search among his acquaintance for ingenuous, well-disposed youths, to whom, with prudent caution, the scheme should be gradually communicated. The members should engage to afford their advice, assistance, and support to each other in promoting one another's interests, business, and advancement in life.

For distinction, we should be called *The Society of the Free and Easy*: free as being, by the practice and habit of the virtues, free from the dominion of vice. And particularly by the practice of industry and frugality, free from debt, which exposes a man to confinement and a species of slavery to his creditors.

This is as much as I can now recollect of the project, except that I communicated it in part to two young men who adopted it with some enthusiasm. But my then narrow circumstances, and the necessity I was under of sticking close to my business, occasioned my postponing the prosecution of it.

My multifarious occupations induced me to continue postponing, so that it has been omitted till I have no longer strength or activity left sufficient for such an enterprise, though I am still of opinion that it was a practicable scheme and might have been very useful by forming a great number of good citizens.

I was not discouraged by the magnitude of the undertaking, as I have always thought that one man of tolerable abilities may work great changes and accomplish great affairs among mankind if he first forms a good plan, and, cutting off all amusements or employments that would divert his attention, makes the execution of that plan his sole study and business.

Chapter 10:
Poor Richard's Almanac and Other Activities

In 1732 I first published my Almanac under the name of *Richard Saunders*. It was continued by me about twenty-five years, commonly called *Poor Richard's Almanac*. I endeavored to make it both entertaining and useful, and it came to be in such demand, that I reaped considerable profit from it, vending annually near ten thousand.

Observing that it was generally read, scarce any neighborhood in the province being without it, I considered it as a proper vehicle for conveying instruction among the common people who bought scarcely any other books. I therefore filled all the little spaces between the remarkable days in the calendar with proverbial sentences, chiefly such as taught industry and frugality, as the means of procuring wealth, and thereby securing virtue, for *it is hard for an empty sack to stand upright*.

These proverbs, which contained the wisdom of many ages and nations, I assembled into a connected discourse prefixed to the Almanac of 1757, as the harangue of a wise old man to the people attending an auction. Bringing all these scattered councils into a focus enabled them to make greater impression. The piece was copied in all the newspapers of the Continent and reprinted in Britain on a broadside, to be stuck up in houses. Two translations were made of it in French.

Great numbers were bought by the clergy and gentry to distribute gratis among their poor parishioners and tenants. In Pennsylvania, as it discouraged useless expense in foreign superfluities, some thought it had its share of influence in producing plenty of money which was observable for several years after its publication.

I considered my newspaper as another means of communicating instruction and frequently reprinted extracts from the Spectator and other moral writers, and I sometimes published little pieces of my own which had been first composed for reading in our Junto. Of these are a Socratic dialogue, tending to prove that, whatever might be his parts and abilities, a vicious man could not properly be called a man of sense. A discourse on self-denial showed that virtue was not secure till its practice became a habit and was free from the opposition of contrary inclinations.

In my newspaper I carefully excluded all libel and personal abuse which has become so disgraceful to our country. Whenever I was solicited to insert anything of that kind, and the writers generally pleaded the liberty of the press, and that a newspaper was like a stage-coach in which anyone who would pay had a right to a place, my answer was that I would print the piece separately if desired, and the author might have as many copies as he pleased to distribute himself.

I would not take upon me to spread his detraction. Having contracted with my subscribers to furnish them with what might be either useful or entertaining, I could not fill their papers with private altercation, in which they had no concern, without doing them injustice.

Many printers make no scruple of gratifying the malice of individuals by false accusations of the fairest characters among ourselves, augmenting animosity even to the producing of duels. They are even so indiscreet as to print scurrilous reflections on the government of neighboring states, and even on the conduct of our best national allies, which may be attended with the most pernicious consequences.

These things I mention as a caution to young printers, that they may be encouraged not to pollute their presses and disgrace their profession by such infamous practices, but refuse steadily, as they may see by my example that such a course of conduct will not, on the whole, be injurious to their interests.

In 1733 I sent one of my journeymen to Charleston, South Carolina, where a printer was wanting. I furnished him with a press and letters, on an agreement of partnership, by which I was to receive one-third of the profits of the business, paying one-third of the expense. He was a man of learning, and honest but ignorant in matters of account. And though he sometimes made me remittances, I could get no account from him, nor any satisfactory state of our partnership while he lived.

On his decease, the business was continued by his widow, who, being born and bred in Holland, where the knowledge of accounts is part of female education, she not only sent me as clear a state as she could find of the transactions past, but continued to account with the greatest regularity and exactness every quarter afterward. She managed the business with such success that she not only brought up reputably a family of children, but was able to purchase of me the printing-house and establish her son in it.

I mention this affair to recommend that education for females in accounting is likely to be of more use to them and their children, in case of widowhood, than either music or dancing. Such knowledge will preserve them from losses imposed by crafty men and enable them to continue a business till a son is grown up fit to go on with it, to the lasting advantage of the family.

About the year 1734 there arrived among us from Ireland a young Presbyterian preacher named Hemphill who delivered with a good voice, and apparently extempore, most excellent discourses, which drew together considerable numbers of different persuasions. I became one of his constant hearers, his sermons pleasing me, as they had little of the dogmatical kind, but inculcated strongly the practice of virtue, or what in the religious stile are called good works.

Those of our congregation who considered themselves orthodox Presbyterians disapproved his doctrine. They were joined by most of the old clergy, who arraigned him of heterodoxy before the synod in order to silence him. I became his zealous partisan and contributed all I could to raise a party in his favor, and we combated for him awhile with some hopes of success. There was much scribbling pro and con upon the occasion.

Finding that, though an elegant preacher, he was but a poor writer, I lent him my pen and wrote for him two or three pamphlets, and one piece in the Gazette of April, 1735. Those pamphlets, as is generally the case with controversial writings, though eagerly read at the time, were soon out of vogue.

During the contest an unlucky occurrence hurt his cause exceedingly. One of our adversaries heard him preach a sermon that was much admired and thought he had somewhere read the sermon before. On search, he found a part quoted at length, in one of the British Reviews, from a discourse of Dr. Foster's.

This detection gave many of our party disgust, who accordingly abandoned his cause, and occasioned our more speedy discomfiture in the synod. I stuck by him, however, as I approved his giving us good sermons composed by others, than bad ones of his own manufacture.

He afterward acknowledged to me that none of those he preached were his own, adding that his memory was such as enabled him to retain and repeat any sermon after one reading only. On our defeat, he left us in search elsewhere of better fortune.

I had begun in 1733 to study languages; I soon made myself so much a master of the French as to be able to read the books with ease. I then undertook Italian. An acquaintance who was also learning it used to tempt me to play chess with him. Finding this took up too much of my study time, I refused to play unless the victor in every game should have a right to impose a task, either in parts of the grammar to be got by heart, or in translations. The vanquished was to perform the task before our next meeting. As we played pretty equally, we thus beat one another into that language. I afterward also acquired enough Spanish to read their books also.

I had only one year's instruction in a Latin school, and that when very young, after which I neglected that language entirely. But when I attained an acquaintance with the French, Italian, and Spanish, I was surprised to find, on looking over a Latin Testament, that I understood much more of that language than I had imagined. This encouraged me to apply myself again to the study of it, and I met with more success, as those preceding languages had greatly smoothed my way.

From these circumstances, I have thought that there is some inconsistency in our common mode of teaching languages. We are told that it is proper to begin first with the Latin, and, having acquired that, it will be more easy to attain those modern languages which are derived from it; and yet we do not begin with the Greek, in order more easily to acquire the Latin.

If you can get to the top of a staircase without using the steps, you will more easily gain them in descending. But certainly, if you begin with the lowest you will with more ease ascend to the top. I therefore offer it to the consideration of those who superintend the education of our youth, whether, since many of those who begin with the Latin, and what they have learnt becomes almost useless, it would not have been better to have begun with the French or Italian. After spending the same time, they would have acquired another tongue or two, that, being in modern use, might be serviceable to them in common life.

After ten years' absence from Boston, and having become easy in my circumstances, I made a journey there to visit my relations. I called at Newport to see my brother and settled there with his printing-house. Our former differences were forgotten, and our meeting was cordial and affectionate.

He was fast declining in his health and requested that, in case of his death, I would take home his son, then but ten years of age, and bring him up to the printing business. This I accordingly performed, sending him a few years to school before I took him into the office. His mother carried on the business till he was grown up, when I assisted him with an assortment of new types. Thus I made my brother ample amends for the service I had deprived him of by leaving him so early.

In 1736 I lost one of my sons, a fine boy of four years old, by the small-pox, taken in the common way. I bitterly regret that I had not given it to him by inoculation. This I mention for the sake of parents who omit that operation on the supposition that they should never forgive themselves if a child died under it. My example shows that the regret may be the same either way, and therefore the safer should be chosen.

Our club, the Junto, was found so useful, and afforded such satisfaction to the members, that several were desirous of introducing their friends, which could not well be done without exceeding the number of twelve that we had settled on as convenient. We had from the beginning made it a rule to keep our institution a secret, which was pretty well observed. The intention was to avoid applications of improper persons for admittance, some of whom we might find it difficult to refuse.

I was one of those against any addition to our number. Instead, I made in writing a proposal that every member separately should form a subordinate club with the same rules, and without informing them of the connection with the Junto. The Junto member was to report what passed in his separate club, and the advantages would include the promotion of our particular interests in business by more extensive recommendation, the increase of our influence in public affairs, and our power of doing good by spreading through the several clubs the sentiments of the Junto.

The project was approved, and every member undertook to form his club, but they did not all succeed. Five or six only were completed. They were useful to themselves, and afforded us a good deal of amusement, information, and instruction, besides answering our views of influencing the public opinion on particular occasions.

My first promotion was my being chosen, in 1736, clerk of the General Assembly. The choice was made that year without opposition, but the year following, a new member made a long speech against me in order to favor some other candidate. I was, however, chosen, which was agreeable to me. Besides the pay for the immediate service as clerk, the place gave me a better opportunity to keep up an interest among the members, which secured to me the business of printing the votes, laws, paper money, and other jobs for the public.

I therefore did not like the opposition of this new member, who was a gentleman of fortune and education, with talents that were likely to give him great influence in the House. I did not, however, aim at gaining his favor by paying any servile respect to him, but, after some time, took this other method.

Having heard that he had in his library a certain very scarce and curious book, I wrote a note to him expressing my desire of perusing that book, and requesting he would do me the favor of lending it to me. He sent it immediately, and I returned it in about a week with another note, expressing strongly my sense of the favor. When we next met in the House, he spoke to me (which he had never done before), and with great civility. He ever after manifested a readiness to serve me on all occasions, so that we became great friends, and our friendship continued to his death.

This is another instance of the truth of an old maxim which says, *"He that has once done you a kindness will be more ready to do you another, than he whom you yourself have obliged."* It shows how much more profitable it is prudently to remove, than to resent, return, and continue inimical proceedings.

In 1737, Colonel Spotswood, late governor of Virginia and then postmaster-general, being dissatisfied with the conduct of his deputy at Philadelphia, took from him the commission and offered it to me. I accepted it readily, and found it of great advantage. Though the salary was small, it facilitated the correspondence that improved my newspaper, increased the number demanded, as well as the advertisements to be inserted, so that it came to afford me a considerable income.

My old competitor's newspaper declined proportionately, and I was satisfied without retaliating his refusal, while postmaster, to permit my papers being carried by the riders. Thus he suffered greatly from his neglect in due accounting, and I mention it as a lesson to those young men who may be employed in managing affairs for others, that they should always render accounts, and make remittances, with great clearness and punctuality. The character of observing such a conduct is the most powerful of all recommendations to new employments and increase of business.

Chapter 11:
Interest in Public Affairs

I began now to turn my thoughts to public affairs. The city watch was one of the first things I conceived to want regulation. It was managed by the constables of the respective wards in turn, and the constable warned a number of housekeepers to attend him for the night. Those who chose to never attend paid him six shillings a year to be excused, which was supposed to be for hiring substitutes, but was much more than necessary for that purpose, and made the constableship a place of profit.

The constable, for a little drink, often got such ragamuffins about him that respectable housekeepers did not choose to mix with them. Walking the rounds, too, was often neglected, and most of the nights spent in tippling.

I wrote a paper to be read in Junto about these irregularities, insisting particularly on the inequality of this six-shilling tax, since a poor widow whose property did not exceed the value of fifty pounds paid as much as the wealthiest merchant who had thousands of pounds worth of goods in his stores.

I proposed as a more effectual watch, the hiring of proper men to serve constantly in that business, and as a more equitable way of supporting the charge, a tax that should be proportioned to the property. This idea, being approved by the Junto, was communicated to the other clubs. The plan was not immediately carried out, but preparing the minds of people for the change paved the way for the law obtained a few years after, when the members of our clubs were grown into more influence.

About this time I wrote a paper (read in Junto, but afterward published) on the different accidents and carelessness by which houses were set on fire, with cautions against them, and means proposed of avoiding them. This gave rise to a project of forming a company to extinguish fires, and mutual assistance in removing and securing goods when in danger.

Thirty associates in this scheme were presently found. Our articles of agreement obliged every member to keep always in good order, a certain number of leather buckets with strong bags and baskets for packing and transporting of goods, which were to be brought to every fire. We agreed to meet once a month and spend a social evening together to communicate such ideas as occurred to us upon the subject of fires, as might be useful in our conduct on such occasions.

The utility of this institution was soon evident and many more desired to be admitted than we thought convenient for one company. They were advised to form another. One new company formed after another, till they became so numerous as to include most of the inhabitants who were men of property.

At the time of my writing this, though fifty years since its establishment, the Union Fire Company still flourishes, though the first members are all deceased but myself and one other. The small fines that have been paid by members for absence at the monthly meetings have been applied to the purchase of fire-engines, ladders, fire-hooks, and other implements for each company.

I question whether there is a city in the world better provided with the means of putting a stop to conflagrations. In fact, since these institutions, the city has never lost by fire more than one or two houses at a time, and the flames have often been extinguished before the house in which they began has been half consumed.

In 1739 Reverend George Whitefield arrived from Ireland. An itinerant preacher, he was at first permitted to preach in some of our churches, but the clergy took a dislike to him and soon refused him their pulpits. He was obliged to preach in the fields where enormous multitudes of all sects and denominations attended his sermons.

I observed the extraordinary influence of his oratory on his hearers, and how much they admired and respected him, notwithstanding his abuse by assuring them they were naturally *half beasts and half devils*. It was wonderful to see the change soon made in the manners of our inhabitants. From being thoughtless or indifferent about religion, it seemed as if all the world were growing religious, so that one could not walk through the town in an evening without hearing psalms sung in different families of every street.

And it being found inconvenient to assemble in the open air, the building of a house to meet in was proposed and persons appointed to receive contributions sufficient to procure the ground and erect a building one hundred feet long and seventy broad, about the size of Westminster Hall. The work was carried on with such spirit as to be finished in a much shorter time than could have been expected. Both house and ground were vested in trustees, expressly for the use of any preacher of any religious persuasion who might desire to say something to the people at Philadelphia.

Mr. Whitefield, in leaving us, went preaching all the way through the colonies to Georgia. Settlement of that province had lately been begun, but instead of being made with hardy, industrious husbandmen accustomed to labor, it was with families of broken shop-keepers, insolvent debtors, and many of indolent and idle habits taken out of the jails, who, being set down in the woods, unqualified for clearing land, and unable to endure the hardships of a new settlement, perished in numbers, leaving many helpless children unprovided for.

The sight of their miserable situation inspired the benevolent heart of Mr. Whitefield with the idea of building an Orphan House there. Returning northward, he preached up this charity and made large collections, for his eloquence had a wonderful power over the hearts and purses of his hearers, of which I myself was an instance.

I did not disapprove of the design, but as Georgia was destitute of materials and workmen, and it was proposed to send them from Philadelphia at a great expense, I thought it would have been better to have built the house here, and brought the children to it. This I advised, but he was resolute in his first project, rejected my counsel, and I therefore refused to contribute.

I happened soon after to attend one of his sermons, in the course of which I perceived he intended to finish with a collection, and I silently resolved he should get nothing from me. I had in my pocket a handful of copper money, three or four silver dollars, and five pistoles in gold. As he proceeded I began to soften, and concluded to give the coppers. Another stroke of his oratory made me ashamed of that, and determined me to give the silver. He finished so admirably, that I emptied my pocket wholly into the collector's dish, gold and all.

At this sermon there was also one of our club, who, being of my sentiments respecting the building in Georgia, and suspecting a collection might be intended, had, by precaution, emptied his pockets before he came from home. Toward the conclusion of the discourse, however, he felt a strong desire to give, and applied to a neighbor who stood near him, to borrow some money for the purpose. The application was to perhaps the only man in the company who had the firmness not to be affected by the preacher. His answer was, "*At any other time, Friend Hopkinson, I would lend to thee freely; but not now, for thee seems to be out of thy right senses.*"

Some of Mr. Whitefield's enemies supposed that he would apply these collections to his own private emolument. But I was intimately acquainted with him, being employed in printing his Sermons and Journals, and never had the least suspicion of his integrity. He was in all his conduct a perfectly *honest man*, and methinks my testimony in his favor ought to have the more weight, as we had no religious connection. He used to pray for my conversion, but never had the satisfaction of believing that his prayers were heard. Ours was a mere civil friendship, sincere on both sides, and lasted to his death.

The following instance will show something of the terms on which we stood. Upon one of his arrivals from England at Boston, he wrote to me that he should come soon to Philadelphia, but knew not where he could lodge when there, as he understood his old friend and host, Mr. Benezet was removed to Germantown.

My answer was, "You know my house; if you can make shift with its scanty accommodations, you will be most heartily welcome."

He replied that if I made that kind offer for Christ's sake, I should not miss of a reward. And I returned, "Don't let me be mistaken; it was not for Christ's sake, but for your sake."

The last time I saw Mr. Whitefield was in London, when he consulted me about his Orphan House concern, and his purpose of appropriating it to the establishment of a college. He had a loud and clear voice, and articulated his words and sentences so perfectly, that he might be heard and understood at a great distance.

He preached one evening from the top of the Courthouse steps, which are in the middle of Market-street, and on the west side of Second-street, which crosses it at right angles. Both streets were filled with his hearers to a considerable distance. Being among the hindmost in Market-street, I had the curiosity to learn how far he could be heard, by retiring backwards down the street towards the river, and I found his voice distinct till I came near Front-street, when some noise in that street obscured it.

Imagining then a semicircle, of which my distance should be the radius, and that it were filled with auditors, to each of whom I allowed two square feet, I computed that he might well be heard by more than thirty thousand. This reconciled me to the newspaper accounts of his having preached to twenty-five thousand people in the fields, and to the ancient histories of generals haranguing whole armies, of which I had sometimes doubted.

By hearing him often, I came to distinguish easily between sermons newly composed, and those which he had often preached. His delivery of the latter was so improved by frequent repetitions that every accent, every emphasis, every modulation of voice, was so perfectly well turned and well placed, that, without being interested in the subject, one could not help being pleased with the discourse; a pleasure of much the same kind received from an excellent piece of music. This is an advantage itinerant preachers have over those who are stationary, as the latter cannot well improve their delivery of a sermon by so many rehearsals.

His writing and printing from time to time gave great advantage to his enemies. Unguarded expressions and erroneous opinions delivered in preaching might have been afterwards explained or qualified. Or they might have been denied, but *litera scripta manet*. Critics attacked his writings violently, and with so much appearance of reason as to diminish the number of his followers. I think if he had never written anything, he would have left behind him a much more numerous and important sect, and his reputation might in that case have been still growing, even after his death, as there being nothing of his writing to censure and give him a lower character. His proselytes would be left at liberty to feign for him as great a variety of excellences they might wish him to have possessed.

My business was now continually augmenting, and my circumstances growing easier. My newspaper became very profitable and for a time almost the only one in this and the neighboring provinces. I experienced the truth of the observation that "*After getting the first hundred pound, it is more easy to get the second*," money itself being of a prolific nature.

The partnership at Carolina having succeeded, I was encouraged to engage in others, and to promote several of my workmen by establishing them with printing-houses in different colonies, on the same terms with that in Carolina. Most of them did well, being enabled at the end of our term, six years, to purchase the types of me and go on working for themselves, by which means several families were raised. Partnerships often finish in quarrels, but mine were all carried on amicably, owing, I think, to the precaution of having very explicitly settled everything to be done by or expected from each partner, so that there was nothing to dispute.

This precaution I recommend to all who enter into partnerships. Whatever esteem and confidence partners may have for each other at the time of the contract, little jealousies and disgusts may arise, with ideas of inequality in the care and burden of the business. These are often attended with breach of friendship and of the connection, perhaps with lawsuits and other disagreeable consequences.

Chapter 12:
Defense of the Province

I had abundant reason to be satisfied with being established in Pennsylvania. However, I regretted there being no provision for defense, nor for a complete education of youth—no militia, nor any college. I therefore, in 1743, drew up a proposal for establishing an academy. Thinking the Reverend Mr. Peters, who was out of employ, a fit person to superintend such an institution, I communicated the project to him. But he declined the undertaking and I let the scheme lie dormant. I succeeded better the next year in establishing a Philosophical Society.

With respect to defense, Spain having been several years at war against Great Britain, and being at length joined by France, brought us into great danger. And the endeavor of our governor, Thomas, to prevail with our Quaker Assembly to pass a militia law, proved abortive. I determined to try what might be done by a voluntary association of the people. To promote this, I first wrote and published a pamphlet, entitled *Plain Truth*, in which I stated our defenseless situation in strong lights, with the necessity of union and discipline for our defense, and promised to propose in a few days an association for that purpose.

The pamphlet had a sudden and surprising effect. I was called upon for the instrument of association, settled the draft of it with a few friends, and set a meeting of the citizens in the large building before mentioned. The house was pretty full. I had prepared printed copies and provided pens and ink dispersed all over the room. I harangued them a little on the subject, read the paper and explained it, and then distributed the copies, which were eagerly signed.

When the papers were collected, we found above twelve hundred hands; and, other copies being dispersed in the country, the subscribers amounted to about ten thousand. These all furnished themselves as soon as they could with arms, formed themselves into companies and regiments, chose their own officers, and met every week to be instructed in military discipline. The women provided silk colors which they presented to the companies, painted with different devices and mottos, which I supplied.

The officers of the companies composing the Philadelphia regiment chose me for their colonel. I declined that station and recommended Mr. Lawrence, a fine person and man of influence, who was accordingly appointed. I then proposed a lottery to defray the expense of building a battery below the town and furnishing it with cannon. It was soon erected, being framed of logs and filled with earth. We bought some old cannon from Boston and wrote to England for more.

Meanwhile, Colonel Lawrence, William Allen, Abram Taylor, Esqr., and myself were sent to New York by the associators, commissioned to borrow some cannon of Governor Clinton. He at first refused, but at dinner with his council, where there was great drinking of Madeira wine, he softened by degrees and said he would lend us six. After a few more bumpers he advanced to ten, and at length he very good-naturedly conceded eighteen. They were fine cannon, eighteen-pounders, with their carriages, which we soon transported and mounted on our battery, where the associators kept a nightly guard while the war lasted, and among the rest I regularly took my turn of duty there as a common soldier.

My activity in these operations was agreeable to the governor and council. They took me into confidence, and I was consulted by them in every measure wherein their concurrence was thought useful to the association. Calling in the aid of religion, I proposed proclaiming a fast to promote reformation and implore the blessing of Heaven on our undertaking.

They embraced the motion, but it was the first fast ever thought of in the province and the secretary had no precedent from which to draw the proclamation. My education in New England, where a fast is proclaimed every year, was here of some advantage: I drew it in the accustomed style, it was translated into German, printed in both languages, and divulged through the province. This gave the clergy of the different sects an opportunity of influencing their congregations to join in the association, and it would probably have been general among all but Quakers if peace had not soon intervened.

It was thought by some of my friends that, by my activity in these affairs, I should offend the Quakers and thereby lose my interest in the Assembly of the province, where they formed a great majority. A young gentleman who wished to succeed me as their clerk, acquainted me that it was decided to displace me at the next election; and he, therefore, in good will, advised me to resign. My answer was that I knew of some public man who made it a rule never to ask for an office, and never to refuse one when offered to him. "I approve," says I, "of his rule, and will practice it with a small addition: I shall never *ask*, never *refuse*, nor ever *resign* an office.

I heard no more of this and was chosen unanimously as usual at the next election. They might have been pleased if I would voluntarily have left them, but they did not care to displace me on account merely of my zeal for the association. Indeed I had cause to believe that the defense of the country was not disagreeable to any of them, provided they were not required to assist in it. And I found that many of them, though against offensive war, were clearly for the defensive.

A transaction in our fire company gave me some insight into their sentiments. It had been proposed that we should build a battery, but by our rules, no money could be disposed of till the next meeting after the proposal. The company consisted of thirty members, of which twenty-two were Quakers, and eight of other persuasions. We eight attended the meeting. We thought some of the Quakers would join us, but only Mr. James Morris appeared to oppose the measure.

While we were disputing this, a waiter came to tell me two gentlemen below desired to speak with me. I went down and found two of our Quaker members who told me eight of them were assembled at a tavern and were determined to come and vote with us if there should be occasion.

Now secure of a majority, I went up, and after a little seeming hesitation, agreed to delay the vote another hour in case those in agreement with Mr. Morris should arrive. Not one of his friends appeared, at which he expressed great surprise. At the end of the hour, we carried the resolution eight to one. As eight of the twenty-two Quakers were ready to vote with us, and thirteen, by their absence, manifested that they were not inclined to oppose the measure, I estimated the proportion of Quakers sincerely against defense as only one in twenty-one.

My being many years in the Assembly, the majority of which were constantly Quakers, gave me frequent opportunities to see the embarrassment given them by their principle against war. Whenever application was made to them by order of the crown to grant aid for military purposes, they were unwilling to offend either government by a direct refusal, or their friends the Quakers by compliance contrary to their principles. The common solution was to grant money under the phrase of its being "*for the king's use*," and never to inquire how it was applied.

But, if the demand was not directly from the crown, that phrase was not proper and some other was invented. When powder was wanting (I think it was for the garrison at Louisburg), and the government of New England solicited a grant from Pennsylvania, they could not grant money to buy powder, because that was an ingredient of war. They voted an aid to New England of three thousand pounds, to be put into the hands of the governor, and appropriated it for the purchasing of bread, flour, wheat or *other grain*.

Some of the council, desiring to give the House still further embarrassment, advised the governor not to accept provision, as not being the thing he had demanded. He replied, "I shall take the money, for I understand very well their meaning; other grain is gunpowder."

When in our fire company I once said to my friend Mr. Syng, one of our members, "Let us move the purchase of a fire-engine; the Quakers can have no objection to that; and then we will buy a great gun, which is certainly a *fire-engine*."

"I see," says he, "you have improved by being so long in the Assembly; your equivocal project would be just a match for their wheat or *other grain*."

The embarrassment the Quakers suffered reminds me of what I think a more prudent conduct in another sect among us, the Dunkers. One of its founders, Michael Welfare, complained that they were grievously calumniated by the zealots of other persuasions, and charged with abominable principles and practices to which they were utter strangers. I told him this had always been the case with new sects, and that, to put a stop to such abuse, it might be well to publish the articles and rules of their belief.

He said it had been proposed among them, but not agreed to, for this reason: "When we were first drawn together as a society," says he, "it had pleased God to enlighten our minds so far as to see that some doctrines, which we once esteemed truths, were errors; and that others, which we had esteemed errors, were real truths. From time to time He has been pleased to afford us farther light, and our principles have been improving, and our errors diminishing. We fear that, if we should once print our confession of faith, we should feel ourselves as if bound and confined by it, and perhaps be unwilling to receive further improvement."

This modesty in a sect is perhaps a singular instance in the history of mankind, every other sect supposing itself in possession of all truth, and that those who differ are wrong; like a man traveling in foggy weather: He appears wrapped up in a fog to those at some distance from him, but near him all appears clear, though in truth he is as much in the fog as any of them. To avoid this kind of embarrassment, the Quakers have of lately been gradually declining in public service, choosing rather to quit their power than their principle.

In 1742 I invented an open stove for the better warming of rooms, and at the same time saving fuel. I made a present of the model to Mr. Robert Grace who, having an iron-furnace, found the casting of the plates for these stoves a profitable thing. To promote demand, I wrote and published a pamphlet, entitled "*An Account of the new-invented Pennsylvania Fireplaces; wherein their Construction and Manner of Operation is particularly explained; their Advantages above every other Method of warming Rooms demonstrated; and all Objections that have been raised against the Use of them answered and obviated.*"

This pamphlet had a good effect. Gov'r. Thomas was so pleased with this stove that he offered to give me a patent for the sole vending of them for a term of years. I declined it from a principle which has ever weighed with me: *That, as we enjoy great advantages from the inventions of others, we should be glad of an opportunity to serve others by any invention of ours; and this we should do freely and generously.*

An ironmonger in London however, assuming a good deal of my pamphlet, and working it up into his own, made some small changes in the machine, which rather hurt its operation, got a patent for it there, and made a little fortune by it. This is not the only instance of patents taken out for my inventions by others, though not always with the same success. I never contested them as I have no desire to profit by patents myself, and I hate disputes. The use of these fireplaces in many houses has been a great saving of wood to the inhabitants.

Chapter 13:
Public Services and Duties

Peace being concluded, and the association business therefore at an end, I turned my thoughts again to the affair of establishing an academy. The first step I took was to associate in the design a number of friends, of whom the Junto furnished a good part. The next step was to write and publish a pamphlet entitled *Proposals Relating to the Education of Youth in Pennsylvania*. This I distributed free of charge, and then I began a subscription for opening and supporting an academy. It was to be paid in quotas yearly for five years. By so dividing it, I judged the subscription might be larger, and I believe it was so, amounting to no less than five thousand pounds.

In the introduction to these proposals, I stated their publication as an act of some *public-spirited gentlemen*, avoiding as much as I could the presenting of myself to the public as the author of any scheme for their benefit. The subscribers chose out of their number twenty-four trustees and appointed Mr. Francis, then attorney-general, and myself to draw up constitutions for the government of the academy. A house was hired, masters engaged, and the schools opened, I think, in the same year, 1749.

The scholars increasing fast, the house was soon found too small, and Providence threw into our way a large house ready built, which might well serve our purpose. This was the building erected by the hearers of

Mr. Whitefield, and was obtained for us in the following manner.

The contributions to this building were made by people of different sects, and therefore care was taken in the nomination of trustees that predominance should not be given to any one sect. It was therefore that one of each sect was appointed, one Church-of-England man, one Presbyterian, one Baptist, one Moravian, etc., those, in case of vacancy by death, were to fill it by election from among the contributors.

The Moravian happened not to please his colleagues, and on his death they resolved to have no other of that sect. At length one mentioned me, with the observation that I was merely an honest man, and of no sect at all, which prevailed with them to choose me. The enthusiasm which existed when the house was built had long since abated, and its trustees had not been able to procure fresh contributions for paying the ground-rent and other debts the building had occasioned. I had a good opportunity of negotiating an agreement by which the trustees for the building were to cede it to those of the academy, the latter undertaking to discharge the debt, to keep forever open in the building a large hall for occasional preachers, according to the original intention, and maintain a free-school for the instruction of poor children.

Writings were accordingly drawn, and on paying the debts the trustees of the academy were put in possession of the premises. By dividing the great and lofty hall into stories, and different rooms above and below for the several schools, and purchasing some additional ground, the whole was soon made fit for our purpose, and the scholars moved into the building.

The care and trouble of agreeing with the workmen, purchasing materials, and superintending the work fell upon me. I went through it cheerfully as it did not interfere with my private business, having the year before taken a very able, industrious, and honest partner, Mr. David Hall, with whose character I was well acquainted, as he had worked for me four years. He took off my hands all care of the printing-office, paying me punctually my share of the profits. The partnership continued eighteen years, successfully for us both.

The trustees of the academy, after a while, were incorporated by a charter from the governor; their funds were increased by contributions in Britain and grants of land from the proprietaries, to which the Assembly has since made considerable addition; and thus was established the present University of Philadelphia. I have been continued one of its trustees from the beginning, now near forty years.

When I disengaged myself from private business, by the sufficient though moderate fortune I had acquired, I had secured leisure during the rest of my life for philosophical studies and amusements. I purchased all Dr. Spence's apparatus, who had come from England to lecture here, and I proceeded in my electrical experiments with great alacrity.

But the public, now considering me as a man of leisure, laid hold of me for their purposes. The governor put me into the commission of the peace; the corporation of the city chose me of the common council, and soon after an alderman; and the citizens at large chose me a burgess to represent them in Assembly. This latter station was more agreeable to me, as I was at length tired with sitting there to hear debates, in which, as clerk, I could take no part, and which were often so unentertaining that I was induced to amuse myself with making magic squares or circles, or anything to avoid weariness.

The office of justice of the peace I tried a little, by attending a few courts, and sitting on the bench to hear causes. But finding that more knowledge of the common law than I possessed was necessary to act in that station with credit, I gradually withdrew from it, excusing myself by my being obliged to attend the higher duties of a legislator in the Assembly. My election to this trust was repeated every year for ten years, without my ever asking any elector for his vote, or signifying, either directly or indirectly, any desire of being chosen. On taking my seat in the House, my son was appointed their clerk.

The following year a treaty was to be held with the Indians at Carlisle, and the governor proposed that the House should nominate some of their members as commissioners. The House named the speaker (Mr. Norris) and me, and we went to Carlisle and met the Indians accordingly.

Those people are extremely apt to get drunk, and when so are very quarrelsome and disorderly, so we strictly forbad the selling of any liquor to them. When they complained of this restriction, we told them that if they would continue sober during the treaty, we would give them plenty of rum when business was over. They promised this, and they kept their promise, because they could get no liquor, and the treaty was conducted very orderly, and concluded to mutual satisfaction.

They then claimed and received the rum. This was in the afternoon. They were near one hundred men, women, and children, and were lodged in temporary cabins, built in the form of a square, just without the town. In the evening, hearing a great noise among them, the commissioners walked out to see what was the matter.

We found they had made a great bonfire in the middle of the square. They were all drunk, men and women, quarreling and fighting. Their dark-colored bodies, half naked, seen only by the gloomy light of the bonfire, running after and beating one another with firebrands, accompanied by their horrid yellings, formed a scene resembling our ideas of hell. There was no appeasing the tumult, and we retired to our lodging. At midnight a number of them came thundering at our door, demanding more rum, of which we took no notice.

The next day, aware they had misbehaved, they sent three of their old counselors to make their apology. The orator acknowledged the fault, but laid it upon the rum, and then endeavored to excuse the rum by saying, "*The Great Spirit, who made all things, made everything for some use, and whatever use he designed anything for, that use it should always be put to. Now, when he made rum, he said, 'Let this be for the Indians to get drunk with,' and it must be so.*"

Indeed, if it be the design of Providence to extirpate these savages in order to make room for cultivators of the earth, it seems probable that rum may be the appointed means. It has already annihilated all the tribes who formerly inhabited the sea-coast.

In 1751, Dr. Thomas Bond, a particular friend of mine, conceived the idea of establishing a hospital in Philadelphia (a very beneficent design, which has been ascribed to me, but was originally his), for the reception and cure of poor sick persons, whether inhabitants of the province or strangers. He was zealous to procure subscriptions for it, but the proposal being a novelty in America, and at first not well understood, he met with small success.

At length he came to me with the compliment that he found there was no such thing as carrying a public-spirited project through without my being concerned in it. "For," says he, "I am often asked by those to whom I propose subscribing, have you consulted Franklin upon this business? And what does he think of it? And when I tell them that I have not (supposing it rather out of your line), they do not subscribe."

I enquired into the nature and probable utility of his scheme, and receiving from him a very satisfactory explanation, I not only subscribed to it myself, but engaged heartily in the design of procuring subscriptions from others. Previously, I endeavored to prepare the minds of the people by writing on the subject in the newspapers, which was my usual custom in such cases, but which he had omitted.

The subscriptions afterwards were more free and generous, but I saw they would be insufficient without assistance from the Assembly and therefore proposed to petition for it, which was done. The country members at first objected that the project could only be serviceable to the city, and therefore they doubted whether the citizens would approve of it. I said I had no doubt of our being able to raise two thousand pounds by voluntary donations. This they considered as a most extravagant supposition, and utterly impossible.

On this I formed my plan. I designed a bill that would only become lawful upon the "payment of two thousand pounds, in two yearly payments, to the treasurer of the hospital, to be applied to the founding, building, and finishing of the same."

This condition carried the bill through, for the members who had opposed the grant now conceived they might have the credit of being charitable without the expense. The subscriptions accordingly soon exceeded the requisite sum, and we claimed and received the public gift, which enabled us to carry the design into execution.

A convenient and handsome building was soon erected, and the institution has by constant experience been found useful, and flourishes to this day. I do not remember any of my political manoeuvers, the success of which gave me more pleasure, or wherein, after thinking of it, I more easily excused myself for having made some use of cunning.

About this time the Rev. Gilbert Tennent came to me with a request that I help him procure a subscription for erecting a new meeting-house for a congregation he had gathered among Presbyterians who were originally disciples of Mr. Whitefield. Unwilling to make myself disagreeable to my fellow-citizens by too frequently soliciting their contributions, I absolutely refused.

He then desired I would furnish him with a list of the names of persons I knew by experience to be generous and public-spirited. I thought it would be unbecoming in me and refused also to give such a list. He then desired I would at least give him my advice.

"That I will readily do," said I. "First, I advise you to apply to all those whom you know will give something; next, to those whom you are uncertain whether they will give anything or not, and show them the list of those who have given; and, lastly, do not neglect those who you are sure will give nothing, for in some of them you may be mistaken."

He laughed and thanked me, and said he would take my advice. He did so, for he asked of *everybody*, and he obtained a much larger sum than he expected, with which he erected the very elegant meeting-house that stands in Arch-street.

Our city, though laid out with a beautiful regularity, had the disgrace of suffering those streets to remain long unpaved. In wet weather the wheels of heavy carriages ploughed them into a quagmire, and in dry weather the dust was offensive. I had lived near what was called the Jersey Market and saw with pain the inhabitants wading in mud while purchasing their provisions.

By talking and writing on the subject, I was instrumental in getting the street paved with stone between the market and the bricked foot-pavement that was on each side next the houses. This gave an easy access to the market dry-shod. But the rest of the street not being paved, and whenever a carriage came out of the mud upon this pavement, it shook off and left its dirt upon it, and it was soon covered with mire.

After some inquiry, I found a poor, industrious man who was willing to sweep the pavement twice a week for the sum of sixpence per month, to be paid by each house. I then wrote and printed a paper setting forth the advantages to the neighborhood that might be obtained by this small expense: greater ease in keeping our houses clean, so much dirt not being brought in by people's feet; the benefit to the shops by more custom, as buyers could more easily get at them; and by not having the dust blown in upon their goods.

I sent one of these papers to each house, and in a day or two went round to see who would agree to pay these sixpences; it was unanimously signed, and all the inhabitants of the city were delighted with the cleanliness of the pavement that surrounded the market. This raised a general desire to have all the streets paved and made the people more willing to submit to a tax for that purpose.

After some time I drew a bill for paving the city and brought it to the Assembly. It was just before I went to England, in 1757, and did not pass till I was gone, and with an additional provision for lighting as well as paving the streets. It was by a private person, the late Mr. John Clifton, his giving a sample of the utility of lamps, by placing one at his door, that the people were first impressed with the idea of lighting all the city.

The honor of this public benefit has been ascribed to me, but it belongs truly to that gentleman. I did but follow his example, and have only some merit to claim respecting the form of our lamps, as differing from the globe lamps we were at first supplied with from London. Those we found inconvenient , for they admitted no air below and therefore the smoke did not readily go out above, soon obstructing the light they were intended to afford. Besides the daily trouble of wiping them clean, an accidental stroke on one of them would demolish it.

I therefore suggested composing them of four flat panes with a long funnel above to draw up the smoke, and crevices admitting air below, to facilitate the ascent of the smoke. By this means they were kept clean and did not grow dark in a few hours, and an accidental stroke would generally break but a single pane, easily repaired.

The mention of these improvements puts me in mind of one I proposed, when in London, to Dr. Fothergill, a great promoter of useful projects. I had observed that the streets were never swept, and in wet weather reduced it to mud. It was with great labor that poor people with brooms raked together and took away the slush. The reason given for not sweeping the dusty streets was that the dust would fly into the windows of shops and houses.

An accidental occurrence instructed me how much sweeping might be done in a little time. One morning I found at my door a poor woman sweeping my pavement with a birch broom. She appeared very pale and feeble, as just come out of a sickness. I asked who employed her to sweep there. She said, "Nobody, but I am very poor and in distress, and I sweeps before gentlefolks' doors, and hopes they will give me something."

I bid her sweep the whole street clean, and I would give her a shilling. This was at nine o'clock, and at 12 she came for the shilling. The whole street was swept perfectly clean and all the dust placed in the gutter, which was in the middle, and the next rain washed it away so that the pavement and even the kennel were perfectly clean. I judged that, if the feeble woman could sweep such a street in three hours, a strong man might have done it in half the time.

Here let me remark the convenience of having but one gutter in such a narrow street, running down its middle, instead of two, one on each side. For where all the rain runs from the sides and meets in the middle, it forms a current strong enough to wash away all the mud, but when divided into two channels, it is often too weak to cleanse either.

My proposal, communicated to the good doctor, was as follows: "For the more effectual cleaning and keeping clean the streets of London and Westminster, it is proposed that the several watchmen be contracted with to have the dust swept up in dry seasons, and the mud raked up at other times, each in the several streets and lanes of his round; that they be furnished with brooms and other proper instruments for these purposes, to be kept at their respective stands, ready to furnish the poor people they may employ in the service.

"That in the dry summer months the dust be all swept up into heaps at proper distances, before the shops and windows of houses are usually opened, when the scavengers, with close-covered carts, shall also carry it all away.

"That the mud, when raked up, be not left in heaps to be spread abroad again by the wheels of carriages and trampling of horses, but that the scavengers be provided with bodies of carts, not placed high upon wheels, but low upon sliders, with lattice bottoms, which, being covered with straw, will retain the mud thrown into them, and permit the water to drain from it, whereby it will become much lighter, water making the greatest part of its weight; these bodies of carts to be placed at convenient distances, and the mud brought to them in wheelbarrows; they remaining where placed till the mud is drained, and then horses brought to draw them away."

Requiring the dust to be swept up and carried away before the shops are open is very practicable in the summer when the days are long, for one morning at seven o'clock, I observed not one shop open, though it had been daylight and the sun up above three hours. The inhabitants of London choose voluntarily to live much by candle-light and sleep by sunshine, and yet often complain, a little absurdly, of the duty on candles, and the high price of tallow.

Some may think these trifling matters not worth relating, and though dust blown into the eyes of a single person or into a single shop on a windy day is but of small importance, yet the great number of instances in a populous city give it consequence.

Human felicity is produced not so much by great pieces of good fortune that seldom happen, as by little advantages that occur every day. If you teach a poor young man to shave himself and keep his razor in order, you may contribute more to the happiness of his life than in giving him a thousand guineas. The money may be soon spent and the only regret foolishly consumed it. But in the other case, he escapes the vexation of waiting for barbers, their sometimes dirty fingers, offensive breaths, and dull razors. He shaves when convenient and enjoys the pleasure of its being done with a good instrument.

With these sentiments I have hazarded the preceding pages, hoping they may afford hints which some time or other may be useful to a city I love, and perhaps to some of our towns in America.

Having been employed by the postmaster-general of America as his comptroller in regulating several offices, upon his death in 1753 I was appointed, jointly with Mr. William Hunter, to succeed him, by a commission from the postmaster-general in England. The American office never had hitherto paid anything to that of Britain. We were to have six hundred pounds a year between us if we could make that sum out of the profits of the office.

To do this, a variety of improvements were necessary. Some were at first expensive, so that in the first four years the office became nine hundred pounds in debt to us. But it soon after began to repay us, and before I was displaced, we had brought it to yield *three times* as much revenue to the crown as the post-office of Ireland.

The business of the post-office occasioned my taking a journey to New England, where the College of Cambridge, of their own motion, presented me with the degree of Master of Arts. Yale College, in Connecticut, had before made me a similar compliment. Thus, without studying in any college, I came to partake of their honors. They were conferred in consideration of my improvements and discoveries in the electric branch of natural philosophy.

Chapter 14:
Albany Plan of Union

In 1754, war with France being again apprehended, a congress of commissioners from the different colonies was to be assembled at Albany, there to confer with the chiefs of the Six Nations concerning the means of defending both their country and ours.

Governor Hamilton requested the House to furnish proper presents for the Indians to be given on this occasion and named the speaker (Mr. Norris) and myself to join Mr. Thomas Penn and Mr. Secretary Peters as commissioners to act for Pennsylvania.

We met the other commissioners at Albany about the middle of June. In our way thither, I drew a plan for the union of all the colonies under one government, so far as might be necessary for defense and other general purposes. As we passed through New York, I had there shown my project to Mr. James Alexander and Mr. Kennedy, two gentlemen of great knowledge in public affairs. Fortified by their approbation, I ventured to lay it before the Congress. It then appeared that several of the commissioners had formed plans of the same kind. A question was first taken whether a union should be established, which passed unanimously. A committee was then appointed, one member from each colony, to consider the several plans and report. Mine happened to be preferred, and, with a few amendments, was accordingly reported.

By this plan the general government was to be administered by a president-general, appointed and supported by the crown, and a grand council was to be chosen by the representatives of the people of the several colonies. The debates upon it in Congress went on daily, hand in hand with the Indian business. At length the many objections and difficulties were overcome, the plan was unanimously agreed to, and copies ordered to be transmitted to the Board of Trade and to the assemblies of the provinces.

The assemblies did not adopt it as they all thought there was too much *prerogative* in it, and in England it was judged to have too much of the *democratic*. The Board of Trade therefore did not approve of it, nor recommend it for the approbation of his majesty.

But another scheme was formed whereby the governors of the provinces were to meet and order the raising of troops, building of forts, etc., and to draw on the treasury of Great Britain for the expense, which was afterwards to be refunded by an act of Parliament laying a tax on America.

Being the winter following in Boston, I had much conversation with Governor Shirley upon both the plans. The different and contrary reasons of dislike to my plan makes me suspect that it was really the true medium; and I am still of opinion it would have been happy for both sides of the water if it had been adopted. The colonies, so united, would have been sufficiently strong to have defended themselves. There would then have been no need of troops from England, and the subsequent pretense for taxing America and the bloody contest it occasioned would have been avoided.

Such mistakes are not new; history is full of the errors of states and princes: "Look round the habitable world, how few know their own good, or, knowing it, pursue!" Those who govern, having much business on their hands, do not generally like to take the trouble of considering and carrying into execution new projects. The best public measures are therefore seldom *adopted from previous wisdom, but forced by the occasion.*

Chapter 15:
Quarrels with the Proprietary Governors

In my journey to Boston this year, I met at New York with our new governor, Mr. Morris, just arrived from England, with whom I had been before intimately acquainted. He brought a commission to supersede Mr. Hamilton, who had resigned due to the disputes his instructions subjected him to. Mr. Morris asked if I thought he must expect as uncomfortable an administration.

I said, "No. You may, on the contrary, have a very comfortable one, if you will only take care not to enter into any dispute with the Assembly."

"My dear friend," says he, pleasantly. "How can you advise my avoiding disputes? You know I love disputing. It is one of my greatest pleasures. However, to show the regard I have for your counsel, I promise you I will, if possible, avoid them."

He had some reason for loving to dispute, being eloquent, an acute sophister, and, therefore, generally successful in argumentative conversation. He had been brought up to it from a boy. But I think the practice is not wise, for these disputing, contradicting, and confuting people are generally unfortunate in their affairs. They get victory sometimes, but they never get good will, which would be of more use to them.

We parted, he going to Philadelphia, and I to Boston. In returning, I met at New York with the votes of the Assembly, by which it appeared that, notwithstanding his promise to me, he and the House were already in high contention, and it was a continual battle between them as long as he retained the government.

I had my share of it, for as soon as I got back to my seat in the Assembly, I was put on every committee for answering his speeches and messages. Our answers, as well as his messages, were often tart, and sometimes indecently abusive. As he knew I wrote for the Assembly, one might have imagined that, when we met, we could hardly avoid cutting throats. But he was so good-natured a man that no personal difference between him and me was occasioned by the contest, and we often dined together.

One afternoon, in the height of this public quarrel, we met in the street. "Franklin," says he, "you must go home with me and spend the evening. I am to have some company that you will like." And, taking me by the arm, he led me to his house.

In gay conversation over our wine he joked that he much admired the idea of Sancho Panza [The self-important squire of Don Quixote in Cervantes' romance] who, when it was proposed to give him a government, requested it might be a government of *blacks*, as then, if he could not agree with his people, he might sell them. One of his friends, who sat next to me, says, "Franklin, why do you continue to side with these Quakers? Had not you better sell them? The proprietor would give you a good price."

"The governor," says I, "has not yet *blacked* them enough." He, indeed, had labored hard to blacken the Assembly in all his messages, but they wiped off his coloring as fast as he laid it on, and placed it, in return, thick upon his own face. Finding he was likely to be negrofied himself, he, as well as Mr. Hamilton, grew tired of the contest and quitted the government.

These public quarrels were all owing to our hereditary governors, who, when any expense was to be incurred for the defense of their province, with incredible meanness instructed their deputies to pass no act for levying the necessary taxes unless their vast estates were in the same act expressly excused. The Assemblies for three years held out against this injustice, though constrained to bend at last. At length Captain Denny, who was Governor Morris's successor, ventured to disobey those instructions. But I am too fast with my story: there are still some transactions to be mentioned that happened during the administration of Governor Morris.

War being in a manner commenced with France, the government of Massachusetts Bay projected an attack upon Crown Point and sent Mr. Quincy to Pennsylvania, and Mr. Pownall to New York to solicit assistance. As I was in the Assembly, knew its temper, and was Mr. Quincy's countryman, he applied to me for my influence and assistance. I dictated his address to them, which was well received.

They voted an aid of ten thousand pounds, but the governor refused assent to the bill unless a clause were inserted exempting the proprietary estate from bearing any part of the tax. The Assembly, though very desirous of making their grant to New England effectual, were at a loss how to accomplish it. Mr. Quincy labored hard with the governor to obtain his assent, but he was obstinate.

I then suggested a method of doing the business without the governor, by orders on the trustees of the Loan office, which, by law, the Assembly had the right of drawing. There was, indeed, little money at that time in the office, and therefore I proposed that the orders should be payable in a year, and to bear an interest of five per cent. With these orders I supposed the provisions might easily be purchased.

The Assembly, with very little hesitation, adopted the proposal. The orders were immediately printed, and I was one of the committee directed to sign and dispose of them. The fund for paying them was the interest of all the paper currency then extant in the province upon loan, together with the revenue arising from the excise, which being known to be more than sufficient, they obtained instant credit.

Thus this important affair was by my means completed. Mr. Quincy returned thanks to the Assembly in a handsome memorial, went home highly pleased with this success of his embassy, and ever after bore for me the most cordial friendship.

Chapter 16:
Braddock's Expedition

The British government, not choosing to permit the union of the colonies as proposed at Albany or to trust that union with their defense, sent over General Braddock with two regiments of regular English troops for that purpose. He landed at Alexandria, Virginia, and thence marched to Frederictown, Maryland, where he halted for carriages.

Our Assembly apprehended that he conceived violent prejudices against them and wished me to wait upon him, not as from them, but as postmaster-general. Under this guise I could settle with him the best mode of conducting dispatches between him and the governors of the provinces. My son accompanied me on this journey.

We found the general at Frederictown, waiting impatiently for the return of those he had sent through the back parts of Maryland and Virginia to collect wagons. I stayed with him several days, dined with him daily, and had full opportunity of removing all his prejudices, by the information of what the Assembly had before his arrival actually done, and were still willing to do, to facilitate his operations.

When I was about to depart, twenty-five wagons were brought in, not all of those in serviceable condition. The general and his officers were surprised, declared the expedition impossible, and exclaimed against the ministers for ignorantly landing them in a country destitute of the means of providing the one hundred and fifty wagons needed to convey their stores and baggage.

I happened to say I thought it was pity they had not landed in Pennsylvania, as in that country almost every farmer had his wagon. The general said, "Then you, sir, who are a man of interest there, can probably procure them for us, and I beg you will undertake it."

I asked what terms were to be offered the owners of the wagons, and I desired to put on paper the terms that appeared to me necessary. This I did, and they were agreed to, and a commission and instructions prepared immediately. Those terms I published as soon as I arrived at Lancaster, as follows:

"Advertisement: Lancaster, *April* 26, 1755.

"Whereas, one hundred and fifty wagons, with four horses to each wagon, and fifteen hundred saddle or pack horses, are wanted for the service of his majesty's forces now about to rendezvous at Will's Creek, and his excellency General Braddock having been pleased to empower me to contract for the hire of the same, I hereby give notice that I shall attend for that purpose at Lancaster from this day to next Wednesday evening, and at York from next Thursday morning till Friday evening, where I shall be ready to agree for wagons and teams, or single horses, on the following terms, viz.:

"1. That there shall be paid for each wagon, with four good horses and a driver, fifteen shillings per diem; and for each able horse with a pack-saddle, or other saddle and furniture, two shillings per diem; and for each able horse without a saddle, eighteen pence per diem.

"2. That the pay commence from the time of their joining the forces at Will's Creek, which must be on or before the 20th of May ensuing, and that a reasonable allowance be paid over and above for the time necessary for their travelling to Will's Creek and home again after their discharge.

"3. Each wagon and team, and every saddle or pack horse, is to be valued by indifferent persons chosen between me and the owner; and in case of the loss of any wagon, team, or other horse in the service, the price according to such valuation is to be allowed and paid.

"4. Seven days' pay is to be advanced and paid in hand by me to the owner of each wagon and team, or horse, at the time of contracting, if required, and the remainder to be paid by General Braddock, or by the paymaster of the army, at the time of their discharge, or from time to time, as it shall be demanded.

"5. No drivers of wagons, or persons taking care of the hired horses, are on any account to be called upon to do the duty of soldiers, or be otherwise employed than in conducting or taking care of their carriages or horses.

"6. All oats, Indian corn, or other forage that wagons or horses bring to the camp, more than is necessary for the subsistence of the horses, is to be taken for the use of the army, and a reasonable price paid for the same.

"Note.—My son, William Franklin, is empowered to enter into like contracts with any person in Cumberland county.

"B. Franklin."

"To the inhabitants of the Counties of Lancaster, York, and Cumberland.

"Friends and Countrymen, being occasionally at the camp at Frederic a few days since, I found the general and officers extremely exasperated on account of their not being supplied with horses and carriages, which had been expected from this province, as most able to furnish them; but, through the dissensions between our governor and Assembly, money had not been provided, nor any steps taken for that purpose.

"It was proposed to send an armed force immediately into these counties, to seize as many of the best carriages and horses as should be wanted, and compel as many persons into the service as would be necessary to drive and take care of them.

"I apprehended that the progress of British soldiers through these counties on such an occasion, especially considering the temper they are in, and their resentment against us, would be attended with many and great inconveniences to the inhabitants, and therefore more willingly took the trouble of trying first what might be done by fair and equitable means. The people of these back counties have lately complained to the Assembly that a sufficient currency was wanting; you have an opportunity of receiving and dividing among you a very considerable sum; for, if the service of this expedition should continue, as it is more than probable it will, for one hundred and twenty days, the hire of these wagons and horses will amount to upward of thirty thousand pounds, which will be paid you in silver and gold of the king's money.

"The service will be light and easy, for the army will scarce march above twelve miles per day, and the wagons and baggage-horses, as they carry those things that are absolutely necessary to the welfare of the army, must march with the army, and no faster; and are, for the army's sake, always placed where they can be most secure, whether in a march or in a camp.

"If you are really, as I believe you are, good and loyal subjects to his majesty, you may now do a most acceptable service, and make it easy to yourselves; for three or four of such as cannot separately spare from the business of their plantations a wagon and four horses and a driver, may do it together, one furnishing the wagon, another one or two horses, and another the driver, and divide the pay proportionately between you; but if you do not this service to your king and country voluntarily, when such good pay and reasonable terms are offered to you, your loyalty will be strongly suspected. The king's business must be done; so many brave troops, come so far for your defense, must not stand idle through your backwardness to do what may be reasonably expected from you; wagons and horses must be had; violent measures will probably be used, and you will be left to seek for a recompense where you can find it, and your case, perhaps, be little pitied or regarded.

"I have no particular interest in this affair, as, except the satisfaction of endeavoring to do good, I shall have only my labor for my pains. If this method of obtaining the wagons and horses is not likely to succeed, I am obliged to send word to the general in fourteen days; and I suppose Sir John St. Clair, the hussar, with a body of soldiers, will immediately enter the province for the purpose, which I shall be sorry to hear, because I am very sincerely and truly your friend and well-wisher,

"B. Franklin."

I received of the general about eight hundred pounds to be disbursed in advance-money to the wagon owners. But that sum being insufficient, I advanced upward of two hundred pounds more, and in two weeks the one hundred and fifty wagons, with two hundred and fifty-nine carrying horses were on their march for the camp. The advertisement promised payment according to the valuation, in case any wagon or horse should be lost. The owners, however, alleging they did not know General Braddock, or what dependence might be had on his promise, insisted on my bond for the performance, which I accordingly gave them.

While I was at the camp, supping one evening with the officers of Colonel Dunbar's regiment, he represented to me his concern for the subalterns, who, he said, were generally not in affluence, and could ill afford to lay in the stores that might be necessary in so long a march through a wilderness where nothing was to be purchased. I commiserated their case, and resolved to endeavor procuring them some relief.

I said nothing to him of my intention, but wrote the next morning to the committee of the Assembly, who had the disposition of some public money, warmly recommending the case of these officers and proposing that a present should be sent them of necessaries and refreshments. My son, who had some experience of a camp life, and of its wants, drew up a list for me, which I enclosed in my letter.

The committee approved, and used such diligence that, conducted by my son, the stores arrived at the camp as soon as the wagons. They consisted of twenty parcels, each containing such rations as sugar, butter, tea, old Madeira wine, Jamaica spirits, cured hams, chocolate, white biscuit, dried tongues, rice, raisins, pepper, white wine, white wine vinegar, ground coffee, mustard, and Gloucester cheese.

These twenty parcels were placed on twenty horses, each a present for one officer. They were very thankfully received, and the kindness acknowledged by letters from the colonels in the most grateful terms. The general, too, was highly satisfied with my conduct in procuring him the wagons and readily paid my account of disbursements, thanked me repeatedly, and requested my farther assistance in sending provisions after him.

I undertook this also, and was busily employed in it till we heard of his defeat, advancing for the service of my own money, upwards of one thousand pounds sterling, of which I sent him an account. It came to his hands, luckily for me, a few days before the battle, and he returned me immediately an order on the paymaster for the round sum of one thousand pounds.

This general was, I think, a brave man, and might have made a good officer in some European war. But he had too much self-confidence, too high an opinion of the validity of regular troops, and too mean a one of both Americans and Indians. George Croghan, our Indian interpreter, joined him on his march with one hundred people who might have been of great use to his army as guides and scouts if he had treated them kindly, but he slighted and neglected them, and they gradually left him.

In conversation with him one day, he was giving me an account of his intended progress. "After taking Fort Duquesne," says he, "I am to proceed to Niagara; and, having taken that, to Frontenac, if the season will allow time; and I suppose it will, for Duquesne can hardly detain me above three or four days; and then I see nothing that can obstruct my march to Niagara."

Having before revolved in my mind the long line his army must make in their march by a very narrow road, to be cut for them through the woods and bushes, and also what I had read of a former defeat of fifteen hundred French, who invaded the Iroquois country, I had some doubts.

I ventured only to say, "To be sure, sir, if you arrive well before Duquesne, with these fine troops, so well provided with artillery, that place not yet completely fortified, and as we hear with no very strong garrison, can probably make but a short resistance.

"The only danger I apprehend of obstruction to your march is from ambuscades of Indians, who, by constant practice, are dexterous in laying and executing them; and the slender line, near four miles long, which your army must make, may expose it to be attacked by surprise in its flanks, and to be cut like a thread into several pieces, which, from their distance, cannot come up in time to support each other."

He smiled at my ignorance, and replied, "These savages may, indeed, be a formidable enemy to your raw American militia, but upon the king's regular and disciplined troops, sir, it is impossible they should make any impression."

I was conscious of an impropriety in my disputing with a military man in matters of his profession, and said no more. The enemy, however, let his army advance without interruption till within nine miles of the place;

and then, when more in a body (for it had just passed a river, where the front had halted till all were come over), and in a more open part of the woods than any it had passed, attacked its advanced guard by heavy fire from behind trees and bushes, which was the first intelligence the general had of an enemy's being near him.

This guard being disordered, the general hurried the troops up to assist them, which was done in great confusion of wagons, baggage, and cattle, and presently the fire came upon their flank. The officers, being on horseback, were easily distinguished, picked out as marks, and fell very fast. The soldiers were crowded together in a huddle, having or hearing no orders, and standing to be shot at till two-thirds of them were killed. And then, being seized with a panic, they fled.

The wagoners each took a horse out of his team and scampered. Their example was immediately followed by others so that all the wagons, provisions, artillery, and stores were left to the enemy. The general, being wounded, was brought off with difficulty. His secretary, Mr. Shirley, was killed by his side, and out of eighty-six officers, sixty-three were killed or wounded, and seven hundred and fourteen men killed out of eleven hundred.

These eleven hundred had been picked men from the whole army. The rest had been left behind with Colonel Dunbar who was to follow with the heavier part of the stores, provisions, and baggage.

Those that fled arrived at Dunbar's camp, and the panic they brought with them instantly seized him and all his people. Though he had now above one thousand men, and the enemy who had beaten Braddock did not exceed four hundred Indians and French together, instead of proceeding and endeavoring to recover some of the lost honor, he ordered all the stores and ammunition to be destroyed that he might have more horses to assist his flight to the settlements.

There he was met with requests from the governors of Virginia, Maryland, and Pennsylvania to post his troops on the frontier so as to afford some protection to the inhabitants. But he continued his hasty march through all the country, not thinking himself safe till he arrived in Philadelphia. This whole transaction gave us Americans the first suspicion that our exalted ideas of the prowess of British regulars had not been well founded.

In their first march, too, from their landing till they got beyond the settlements, they had plundered and stripped the inhabitants, totally ruining some poor families, besides insulting, abusing, and confining the people if they remonstrated. This was enough to put us out of conceit of such defenders, if we had really wanted any. How different was the conduct of our French friends in 1781, who, during a march from Rhode Island to Virginia, near seven hundred miles, occasioned not the smallest complaint for the loss of a pig, a chicken, or even an apple.

Captain Orme, one of the general's aids-de-camp, was grievously wounded and brought off with him, and continued with him to his death. He told me that he was totally silent all the first day, and at night only said, *"Who would have thought it?"* He was silent again the following day, saying only at last, *"We shall better know how to deal with them another time,"* and died a few minutes after.

The secretary's papers, with all the general's orders, instructions, and correspondence, fell into the enemy's hands,and they selected and translated into French a number of the articles which they printed to prove the hostile intentions of the British court before the declaration of war. Among these I saw some letters of the general to the ministry, speaking highly of the great service I had rendered the army, and recommending me to their notice.

David Hume [Scotch philosopher and historian], who was some years after secretary to Lord Hertford when minister in France, and afterward to General Conway when secretary of state, told me he had seen among the papers in that office, letters from Braddock highly recommending me. But, the expedition having been unfortunate, my service, it seems, was not thought of much value, for those recommendations were never of any use to me.

As to rewards from himself, I asked only one, which was, that he would give orders not to enlist any more of our bought servants, and that he would discharge such as had been already enlisted. Several were accordingly returned to their masters.

Dunbar, when the command devolved on him, was not so generous. He being at Philadelphia on his retreat, or rather flight, I applied to him for the discharge of the servants of three poor farmers of Lancaster County that he had enlisted, reminding him of the late general's orders. He promised me that, if the masters would come to him at Trenton, where he should be in a few days on his march to New York, he would deliver their men to them. They accordingly were at the expense and trouble of going to Trenton, and there he refused to perform his promise.

As soon as the loss of the wagons and horses was generally known, all the owners came upon me for the valuation which I had given bond to pay. Their demands gave me a great deal of trouble, for while the money was ready in the paymaster's hands, orders for paying it must first be obtained from General Shirley. I had applied to that general by letter, but, he was at a distance and an answer could not soon be received. All this was not sufficient to satisfy, and some began to sue me. General Shirley at length relieved me from this terrible situation by appointing commissioners to examine the claims and ordering payment. They amounted to near twenty thousand pound, which to pay would have ruined me.

Chapter 17:
Defense of the Frontier

I had been active in drawing a bill for establishing and disciplining a voluntary militia, which I carried through the House without much difficulty, as care was taken in it to leave the Quakers at their liberty. To promote the association necessary to form the militia, I wrote a dialogue, stating and answering all the objections I could think of to such a militia, which was printed, and had, as I thought, great effect.

While the several companies in the city and country were forming and learning their exercise, the governor prevailed with me to take charge of our North-western frontier, which was infested by the enemy, and provide for the defense of the inhabitants by raising troops and building a line of forts.

I undertook this military business, though I did not conceive myself well qualified for it. He gave me a commission with full powers, and a parcel of blank commissions for officers to be given to whom I thought fit. I had little difficulty in raising men, having soon five hundred and sixty under my command. My son, who had in the preceding war been an officer in the army raised against Canada, was my aid-de-camp, and of great use to me. The Indians had burned Gnadenhut, a village settled by the Moravians, and massacred the inhabitants, but the place was thought a good situation for a fort.

In order to march there, I assembled the companies at Bethlehem, the chief establishment of those people. I was surprised to find it in so good a posture of defense; the destruction of Gnadenhut had made them apprehend danger. The principal buildings were defended by a stockade. They had purchased arms and ammunition from New York, and had even placed paving stones between the windows of their high stone houses for their women to throw down upon the heads of any Indians that should attempt to force into them.

The armed brethren, too, kept watch, and relieved as methodically as in any garrison town. In conversation with the bishop, Spangenberg, I mentioned my surprise; for, knowing they had obtained an act of Parliament exempting them from military duties in the colonies, I supposed they were conscientiously scrupulous of bearing arms. He answered me that it was not one of their established principles, but that, at the time of their obtaining that act, it was thought to be a principle with many of their people. On this occasion, however, they, found it adopted by but a few. It seems they were either deceived in themselves, or they deceived the Parliament. But common sense, aided by present danger, will sometimes be too strong for whimsical opinions.

In the beginning of January we set out upon this business of building forts. I sent one detachment toward the Minisink, with instructions to erect one for the security of that upper part of the country, and another to the lower part. And I concluded to go myself with the rest of my force to Gnadenhut, where a fort was thought more immediately necessary. The Moravians procured me five wagons for our tools, stores, and baggage.

Just before we left Bethlehem, eleven farmers who had been driven from their plantations by the Indians came to me requesting a supply of firearms that they might go back and fetch off their cattle. I gave them each a gun with suitable ammunition.

We had not marched many miles before it began to rain, and it continued raining all day. There were no habitations on the road to shelter us till we arrived near night at the house of a German, where, and in his barn, we were all huddled together, as wet as water could make us. It was well we were not attacked in our march, for our arms were of the most ordinary sort, and our men could not keep their gun locks dry. The Indians are dexterous in contrivances for that purpose, which we had not. They met that day the eleven poor farmers above mentioned, and killed ten of them. The one who escaped informed that their guns would not go off, the priming being wet with the rain.

The next day being fair, we continued our march and arrived at the desolated Gnadenhut. There was a saw-mill near where several piles of boards were left, and with them we soon hutted ourselves as we had no tents. Our first work was to bury more effectually the dead we found there, who had been half interred by the country people.

The next morning our fort was planned and marked out, the circumference measuring four hundred and fifty-five feet, which would require as many palisades to be made of trees, one with another, of a foot diameter each. Our axes, of which we had seventy, were immediately set to work to cut down trees. Our men were dexterous in the use of them and great dispatch was made.

Seeing the trees fall so fast, I had the curiosity to look at my watch when two men began to cut at a pine, and in six minutes they had it on the ground. I found it to be fourteen inches diameter. Each pine made three palisades of eighteen feet long, pointed at one end.

While these were preparing, our other men dug a trench all round, of three feet deep, in which the palisades were to be planted. We had ten carriages, with two horses each, to bring the palisades from the woods to the spot. When they were set up, our carpenters built a stage of boards all round within, about six feet high, for the men to stand on to fire through the loopholes.

We had one swivel gun, which we mounted on one of the angles and fired it as soon as fixed, to let the Indians know that we had such pieces. Thus our fort, if such a magnificent name may be given to so miserable a stockade, was finished in a week, though it rained so hard every other day that the men could not work.

This gave me occasion to observe that men are best contented when they are employed. On the days they worked they were good-natured and cheerful, and with the consciousness of having done a good day's work, they spent the evening jollily. But on idle days they were mutinous and quarrelsome; finding fault with their pork or bread, and in continual ill-humor, which put me in mind of a sea-captain whose rule it was to keep his men constantly at work. When his mate once told him that they had done everything, and there was nothing further to employ them about, *"Oh," says he, "make them scour the anchor."*

This kind of fort, however contemptible, is a sufficient defense against Indians who have no cannon. Finding ourselves now posted securely, and having a place to retreat, we ventured out in parties to scour the adjacent country. We met with no Indians, but we found the places on the neighboring hills where they had lain to watch our proceedings.

There was an art in their contrivance of those places that seems worth mention. It being winter, a fire was necessary for them, but a common fire on the surface of the ground would by its light have discovered their position at a distance. They had therefore dug holes in the ground about three feet diameter, and somewhat deeper. We saw where they had with their hatchets cut off the charcoal from the sides of burnt logs lying in the woods. With these coals they had made small fires in the bottom of the holes.

We observed among the weeds and grass the prints of their bodies made by their laying all round with their legs hanging down in the holes to keep their feet warm. This kind of fire, so managed, could not discover them, either by its light, flame, sparks, or even smoke. It appeared that their number was not great, and it seems they saw we were too many to be attacked.

We had for our chaplain a zealous Presbyterian minister, Mr. Beatty, who complained to me that the men did not generally attend his prayers and exhortations. When they enlisted, they were promised, besides pay and provisions, a gill of rum a day, which was punctually served out to them, half in the morning, and the other half in the evening. I observed they were punctual in attending to receive it, and I said to Mr. Beatty, "It is, perhaps, below the dignity of your profession to act as steward of the rum, but if you were to deal it out and only just after prayers, you would have them all about you."

He liked the thought, undertook the office, and, with the help of a few hands to measure out the liquor, executed it to satisfaction, and never were prayers more generally and more punctually attended. I thought this method preferable to the punishment inflicted by some military laws for non-attendance on divine service.

I had hardly finished this business, and got my fort well stored with provisions, when I received a letter from the governor that he had called the Assembly and wished my attendance. My three forts being now completed and the inhabitants contented to remain on their farms under that protection, I resolved to return. A New England officer, Colonel Clapham, experienced in Indian war, being on a visit to our establishment, consented to accept the command.

I gave him a commission, and, parading the garrison, had it read before them and introduced him as an officer who, from his skill in military affairs, was more fit to command them than myself. And, giving them a little exhortation, took my leave.

I was escorted to Bethlehem where I rested a few days. The first night, being in a good bed, I could hardly sleep, it was so different from my hard lodging on the floor of our hut wrapped only in a blanket or two.

While at Bethlehem, I inquired a little into the practice of the Moravians. Some of them had accompanied me, and all were very kind to me. I found they worked for a common stock, ate at common tables, and slept in common dormitories. In the dormitories I observed loopholes at certain distances all along just under the ceiling, which I thought judiciously placed for change of air.

I was at their church, where I was entertained with good music, the organ being accompanied with violins, hautboys, flutes, and clarinets. I understood that their sermons were not usually preached to mixed congregations of men, women, and children, as is our common practice, but that they assembled sometimes the married men, at other times their wives, then the young men, the young women, and the little children, each division by itself.

The sermon I heard was to the children, who came in and were placed in rows on benches; the boys under the conduct of a young man, their tutor, and the girls conducted by a young woman. The discourse seemed well adapted to their capacities and was delivered in a pleasing, familiar manner, coaxing them to be good. They behaved very orderly, but looked pale and unhealthy, which made me suspect they were kept too much within doors, or not allowed sufficient exercise.

I inquired concerning the Moravian marriages, whether the report was true that they were by lot. I was told that lots were used only in particular cases. Generally, when a young man found himself disposed to marry, he informed the elders of his class, who consulted the elder ladies that governed the young women. As these elders of the different sexes were well acquainted with the tempers and dispositions of their respective pupils, they could best judge what matches were suitable, and their judgments were generally acquiesced in. But if it should happen that two or three young women were found to be equally proper for the young man, the lot was then recurred to. I objected, if the matches are not made by the mutual choice of the parties, some of them may be very unhappy. "And so they may," answered my informer, "if you let the parties choose for themselves," which, indeed, I could not deny.

In Philadelphia I found the association went on swimmingly. The inhabitants that were not Quakers formed themselves into companies and chose their captains, lieutenants, and ensigns, according to the new law. Dr. B. visited me, and gave me an account of the pains he had taken to spread a general good liking to the law, and ascribed much to those endeavors. I had the vanity to ascribe all to my *Dialogue*; however, not knowing but that he might be in the right, I let him enjoy his opinion.

The officers chose me to be colonel of the regiment, which I accepted. I forget how many companies we had, but we paraded about twelve hundred well-looking men, with a company of artillery furnished with six brass field-pieces which they had become so expert in the use of as to fire twelve times in a minute. The first time I reviewed my regiment they accompanied me to my house and would salute me with some rounds fired before my door, which shook down and broke several glasses of my electrical apparatus. And my new honor proved not much less brittle, for all our commissions were soon after broken by a repeal of the law in England.

During this short time of my colonelship, being about to set out on a journey to Virginia, the officers of my regiment took it into their heads that it would be proper to escort me out of town as far as the Lower Ferry. Just as I was getting on horseback they came to my door, between thirty and forty, mounted, and all in their uniforms. I had not been previously acquainted with the project or I should have prevented it, and I was chagrined at their appearance, as I could not avoid their accompanying me.

What made it worse was that they drew their swords and rode with them naked all the way. Somebody wrote an account of this to the proprietor, and it gave him great offense. No such honor had been paid him, nor to any of his governors, and he said it was only proper to princes of the blood royal, which may be true for aught I know.

This silly affair, however, greatly increased his rancor against me, which was before not a little on account of my conduct in the Assembly respecting the exemption of his estate from taxation, which I had always opposed. He accused me to the ministry as being the great obstacle to the King's service, preventing, by my influence in the House, the proper form of the bills for raising money, and he instanced this parade with my officers as a proof of my having an intention to take the government of the province out of his hands by force.

Notwithstanding the continual wrangle between the governor and the House, we never had any personal difference. His little or no resentment against me might be the effect of professional habit. Being bred a lawyer, he might consider us both as merely advocates for contending clients in a suit, he for the proprietaries and I for the Assembly. He would, therefore, sometimes call in a friendly way to advise with me on difficult points, and sometimes take my advice.

We acted in concert to supply Braddock's army with provisions. When the shocking news arrived of his defeat, the governor sent in haste for me, to consult with him on measures for preventing the desertion of the back counties. And, after my return from the frontier, he would have had me undertake the conduct of such an expedition with provincial troops, and he proposed to commission me as general.

I had not so good an opinion of my military abilities as he professed to have, but probably he might think that my popularity would facilitate the raising of the men, and my influence in Assembly might grant of money to pay them, perhaps without taxing the proprietary estate. Finding me not so forward to engage as he expected, the project was dropped, and he soon after left the government, being superseded by Captain Denny.

Chapter 18:
Scientific Experiments

In 1746, being at Boston, I met there with a Dr. Spence, lately arrived from Scotland, who showed me some electric experiments. They were imperfectly performed, but being on a subject new to me, they surprised and pleased me. Soon after my return to Philadelphia, our library company received from Mr. P. Collinson, Fellow of the Royal Society of London, a present of a glass tube with instructions on the use of it in making such experiments.

I eagerly seized the opportunity of repeating what I had seen at Boston and acquired great readiness in performing those as well as adding a number of new ones as instructed in the material from England. M my house was continually full, for some time, with people who came to see these new wonders.

To divide a little this encumbrance among my friends, I caused a number of similar tubes to be blown at our glass-house, with which they furnished themselves, so that we had at length several performers. The principal was Mr. Kinnersley, an ingenious neighbor who I encouraged to undertake showing the experiments for money. I drew up for him two lectures in which the experiments were ranged in order and accompanied with explanations such that the foregoing should assist in comprehending the following. He procured an elegant apparatus for the purpose, in which all the little machines that I had roughly made for myself were nicely formed by instrument-makers. His lectures were well attended and gave great satisfaction. After some time he went through the colonies, exhibiting them in every capital town, and picked up some money.

Obliged as we were to Mr. Collinson for his present of the tube, I thought it right he should be informed of our success in using it, and wrote him several letters containing accounts of our experiments. He got them read in the Royal Society.

One paper which I wrote for Mr. Kinnersley on the sameness of lightning with electricity, I sent to Dr. Mitchel, an acquaintance of mine and one of the members of that society. He wrote me word that it had been read, but was laughed at by the connoisseurs. The papers, however, being shown to Dr. Fothergill, he thought them of too much value to be stifled, and advised printing them. Mr. Collinson gave them to *Cave* for publication in his Gentleman's Magazine, but he chose to print them separately in a pamphlet, and Dr. Fothergill wrote the preface.

It was some time before those papers were taken notice of in England. A copy of them fell into the hands of the Count de Buffon, a philosopher of great reputation all over Europe. He prevailed with M. Dalibard to translate them into French, and they were printed at Paris. The publication offended the Abbé Nollet, preceptor in Natural Philosophy to the royal family, and an able experimenter, who had published a theory of electricity which then had the general vogue. He could not believe such a work came from America and said it must have been fabricated by his enemies at Paris. After being assured that there really existed such a person as

Franklin at Philadelphia, he published a volume of Letters, chiefly addressed to me, defending his theory, and denying the verity of my experiments.

I never answered M. Nolett on consideration that my writings contained a description of experiments which anyone might repeat and verify, and therefore I saw no need to defend them. And, reflecting that a dispute between two persons writing in different languages might be lengthened by mistranslations and misconceptions, much of one of the abbé's letters being founded on an error in the translation, I concluded to let my papers shift for themselves. The event gave me no cause to repent my silence, for M. le Roy of the Royal Academy of Sciences took up my cause and refuted him. My book was translated into Italian, German, and Latin, and the doctrine it contained was by degrees universally adopted by the philosophers of Europe, in preference to that of the abbé.

What gave my book the more sudden and general celebrity was the success of one of its proposed experiments, made by Messrs. Dalibard and De Lor at Marly, for drawing lightning from the clouds. M. de Lor, who had an apparatus for experimental philosophy and lectured in that branch of science, undertook to repeat what he called the *Philadelphia Experiments.* After they were performed before the king and court, all the curious of Paris flocked to see them. I will not swell this narrative with an account of that capital experiment, nor of the infinite pleasure I received in the success of a similar one I made with a kite at Philadelphia, as both are to be found in the histories of electricity.

Dr. Wright, an English physician, wrote an account of the high esteem my experiments were in among the learned abroad, and wondered that my writings had been so little noticed in England. The celebrated Dr. Watson drew up a summary of them, and of all I had afterwards sent to England on the subject, which he accompanied with some praise of the writer. This summary was printed in the Transactions of the Royal Society, and the very ingenious Mr. Canton verified the experiment of procuring lightning from the clouds by a pointed rod, and acquainted them with the success.

They soon made me more than amends for the slight with which they had before treated me. Without my having made any application for that honor, they chose me a member, voted that I should be excused the customary payments, and ever since have given me their Transactions gratis. They also presented me with the gold medal of Sir Godfrey Copley for the year 1753, the delivery of which was accompanied by a very handsome speech of the president, Lord Macclesfield, wherein I was highly honored.

Chapter 19:
Agent of Pennsylvania in London

Our new governor, Captain Denny, brought over the before mentioned medal from the Royal Society, which he presented to me at an entertainment given him by the city. He accompanied it with polite expressions of his esteem for me, having, as he said, been long acquainted with my character. After dinner, when the company was engaged in drinking, he took me aside and said he had been advised by his friends in England to cultivate a friendship with me. As one capable of giving him the best advice, and of contributing most effectually to making his administration easy, he desired to have a good understanding with me, and he begged me to be assured of his readiness to render me every service that might be in his power.

He said much to me, also, of the proprietor's good disposition towards the province, and of the advantage it might be to us all if the opposition that had so long continued to his measures was dropt, and harmony restored between him and the people. Effecting such changes, it was thought, might be particularly advantageous to me, and I might depend on adequate acknowledgments and recompenses, etc., etc. The drinkers, finding we did not return immediately to the table, sent us a decanter of Madeira, which the governor made liberal use of, and in proportion became more profuse of his solicitations and promises.

My answers were that my circumstances, thanks to God, were such as to make proprietary favors unnecessary. Being a member of the Assembly, I could not possibly accept any. However, I had no personal enmity to the proprietary, and whenever the public measures he proposed should appear to be for the good of the people, no one should espouse and forward them more zealously than myself. I said I was much obliged to him (the governor) for his professions of regard to me, and that he might rely on everything in my power to make his administration as easy as possible. I hoped at the same time that he had not brought with him the same unfortunate instructions that hampered his predecessor.

When he afterwards came to do business with the Assembly, the disputes were renewed, and I was as active as ever in the opposition. But between us personally no enmity arose. We were often together. He was a man of letters, had seen much of the world, and was very entertaining in conversation. He gave me the first information that my old friend Jas. Ralph was still alive, was esteemed one of the best political writers in England, had been employed in the dispute between Prince Frederic and the king, obtained a pension of three hundred a year, his reputation was indeed small as a poet (Pope having damned his poetry in the *Dunciad*), but his prose was thought as good as any man's.

The proprietary persisted in manacling the deputies of the Assembly with instructions inconsistent not only with the privileges of the people, but with the service of the crown, resolved to petition the king against them, and appointed me their agent to go over to England. The House sent up a bill to the governor granting sixty thousand pounds for the king's use (ten thousand pounds of which was subjected to the orders of the general, Lord Loudoun), which the governor refused to pass, in compliance with his instructions.

I had agreed with Captain Morris for my passage, and my stores were put on board, when Lord Loudoun arrived at Philadelphia to endeavor an accommodation between the governor and Assembly, that his majesty's service might not be obstructed by their dissensions. Accordingly, he desired the governor and myself to meet him, that he might hear what was to be said on both sides. We met and discussed the business. I spoke in behalf of the Assembly, and the governor pleaded his instructions, the bond he had given to observe them, and his ruin if he disobeyed, yet seemed willing to hazard himself if Lord Loudoun would advise it. This his lordship did not choose to do, though I once thought I had nearly prevailed with him to do it, but finally he rather chose to urge the compliance of the Assembly.

I acquainted the House with what had passed and presented them with a set of resolutions I had drawn up, declaring our rights, and that we did not relinquish our claim to those rights, but only suspended the exercise of them on this occasion through *force*, against which we protested. They agreed to drop that bill and frame another conformable to the proprietary instructions. This of course the governor passed, and I was then at liberty to proceed on my voyage.

It was about the beginning of April that I came to New York, and due to the tremendous incompetency of Lord Loudoun, which I shall not go into here, I think it was near the end of June before we sailed. Our captain had boasted much of the swiftness of his ship, but when we came to sea, she proved the dullest of ninety-six sail, to his no small mortification. After many conjectures respecting the cause, our captain suspected that she was loaded too much by the head. The casks of water had been all placed forward. These he therefore ordered to be moved further aft, on which the ship recovered her character, and proved the best sailer in the fleet.

The captain said she had once gone at the rate of thirteen knots, which is accounted thirteen miles per hour. We had on board as a passenger Captain Kennedy, of the Navy, who contended that it was impossible, that no ship ever sailed so fast, and that there must have been some error in the division of the log-line.

A wager ensued between the two captains, to be decided when there should be sufficient wind. Kennedy examined rigorously the log-line, and, being satisfied with that, he determined to throw the log himself. Some days after, when the wind blew very fair and fresh, Captain Lutwidge said he believed she then went at the rate of thirteen knots. Kennedy made the experiment and owned his wager lost.

The above fact I give for the sake of the following observation. It has been remarked, as an imperfection in the art of ship-building, that it can never be known, till she is tried, whether a new ship will or will not be a good sailer. The model of a good-sailing ship has been exactly followed in a new one which has proved dull. This may be occasioned by the different opinions of seamen respecting the modes of lading, rigging, and sailing of a ship. Each has his system; and the same vessel, laden by the judgment and orders of one captain, shall sail better or worse than when by the orders of another. It scarce ever happens that a ship is formed, fitted for the sea, and sailed by the same person. One man builds the hull, another rigs her, a third lades and sails her. No one of these has the advantage of knowing all the ideas and experience of the others and cannot draw just conclusions from a combination of the whole.

In the simple operation of sailing when at sea, I have often observed different judgments in the officers who commanded the successive watches, the wind being the same. One would have the sails trimmed sharper or flatter than another, so that they seemed to have no certain rule to govern by. I think a set of experiments might be instituted, first to determine the most proper form of the hull for swift sailing, next the best dimensions and most proper place for the masts, then the form and quantity of sails and their position to the wind, and the disposition of the lading. This is an age of experiments, and I think a set accurately made and combined would be of great use. Ere long some ingenious philosopher will undertake it, to whom I wish success.

We were several times chased in our passage, but out-sailed everything, and in thirty days had soundings. In the morning it was found by the soundings that we were near our port, but a thick fog hid the land . About nine o'clock the fog began to lift up from the water like the curtain at a play-house, discovering underneath the town of Falmouth, the vessels in its harbor, and the fields that surrounded it.

I set out immediately, with my son, for London. We only stopped a little by the way to view Stonehenge on

Salisbury Plain, and Lord Pembroke's house and gardens, with his very curious antiquities at Wilton. We arrived in London the 27th of July, 1757.

As soon as I was settled in a lodging Mr. Charles had provided for me, I went to visit Dr. Fothergill whose counsel I was advised to obtain. He was against an immediate complaint to government and thought the proprietaries should first be personally applied to, who might possibly be induced to accommodate matters amicably. I then waited on my old friend Mr. Peter Collinson, who told me that John Hanbury, the great Virginia merchant, had requested to be informed when I arrived that he might carry me to Lord Granville's, who was then President of the Council and wished to see me as soon as possible. I agreed to go with him the next morning.

The nobleman received me with great civility. After some questions respecting the state of affairs in America, he said, "You Americans have wrong ideas of the nature of your constitution. You contend that the king's instructions to his governors are not laws, and think yourselves at liberty to regard or disregard them at your own discretion. But those instructions are not like the pocket instructions given to a minister going abroad, for regulating his conduct in some trifling point of ceremony. They are first drawn up by judges learned in the laws. They are then considered, debated, and perhaps amended in Council, after which they are signed by the king. They are then, so far as they relate to you, the *law of the land*, for the king is the Legislator of the Colonies."

I told his lordship this was new doctrine to me. I had always understood from our charters that our laws were to be made by our Assemblies, to be presented indeed to the king for his royal assent, but that being once given the king could not repeal or alter them. And as the Assemblies could not make permanent laws without his assent, so neither could he make a law for them without theirs.

He assured me I was totally mistaken. I did not think so. However, alarmed as to what might be the sentiments of the court concerning us, I wrote it down as soon as I returned to my lodgings. I recollected that about 20 years before, a clause in a bill brought into Parliament had proposed to make the king's instructions laws in the colonies, but the clause was thrown out by the Commons, for which we adored them as friends of liberty. From their conduct toward us in 1765 it seems they had refused that point of sovereignty to the king only that they might reserve it for themselves.

With his insight into human nature and knowledge of American character, he foresaw the inevitable result of such an attitude on the part of England. This conversation with Grenville makes these last pages of the *Autobiography* one of its most important parts.

Dr. Fothergill spoke to the proprietaries and they agreed to meet with me at Mr. T. Penn's house in Spring Garden where we then went into consideration of our several points of complaint, which I enumerated.

The proprietaries justified their conduct as well as they could, and I the Assembly's. We now appeared so far from each other in our opinions as to discourage all hope of agreement. However, it was concluded that I should give them the heads of our complaints in writing, and they promised to consider them.

I did so soon, but they put the paper into the hands of their solicitor, Ferdinand John Paris, who managed all their law business in their great suit with the neighboring proprietary of Maryland, Lord Baltimore, which had subsisted 70 years. He was a proud, angry man, and as I had occasionally in the answers of the Assembly treated his papers with some severity, they being really weak in point of argument and haughty in expression, he had conceived a mortal enmity to me.

I declined the proprietary's proposal that he and I should discuss the complaints between our two selves. They then put the paper into the hands of the Attorney and Solicitor-General for their opinion and counsel upon it, where it lay unanswered a year wanting eight days. When they did receive it I never learned, for they did not communicate it to me, but sent a long message to the Assembly drawn and signed by Paris, complaining of my paper's want of formality as rudeness, and giving a flimsy justification of their conduct, adding that they should be willing to accommodate matters if the Assembly would send out *some person of candor*, intimating thereby that I was not such.

The want of formality or rudeness was probably my not having addressed the paper to them with their assumed titles of True and Absolute Proprietaries of the Province of Pennsylvania, which I omitted as not thinking it necessary in a paper, the intention of which was only to reduce to a certainty by writing, what in conversation I had delivered *viva voce*.

During this delay, the Assembly prevailed with Gov'r Denny to pass an act taxing the proprietary estate in common with the estates of the people. However, when this act came over, the proprietaries, counselled by Paris, determined to oppose its receiving the royal assent. Accordingly they petitioned the king in Council, and a hearing was appointed in which two lawyers were employed by them against the act, and two by me in support of it.

They alleged that the act was intended to load the proprietary estate in order to spare those of the people, and that if it were suffered to continue in force, and the proprietaries would inevitably be ruined. We replied that the act had no such intention and would have no such effect. The assessors were honest and discreet men under an oath to assess fairly and equitably, and that any advantage each of them might expect in lessening his own tax by augmenting that of the proprietaries was too trifling to induce them to perjure themselves.

We also insisted strongly on the mischievous consequences that must attend a repeal, for the money, £100,000 being printed and given to the king's use, expended in his service, and now spread among the people, the repeal would strike it dead in their hands to the ruin of many. The selfishness of the proprietors in soliciting such a catastrophe, merely from a groundless fear of their estate being taxed too highly, was insisted on in the strongest terms.

On this, Lord Mansfield beckoned me into the clerk's chamber and asked if I was really of the opinion that no injury would be done the proprietary estate in the execution of the act. I said certainly. "Then," says he, "you can have little objection to enter into an engagement to assure that point."

I answered, "None at all." He then called in Paris, and after some discourse, his lordship's proposition was accepted on both sides. A paper to the purpose was drawn up by the Clerk of the Council, which I signed with Mr. Charles, who was also an Agent of the Province for their ordinary affairs. Lord Mansfield returned to the Council Chamber where finally the law was allowed to pass.

The Assembly looked into my entering into the first part of the engagement as an essential service to the Province since it secured the credit of the paper money then spread over all the country. They gave me their thanks when I returned. But the proprietaries were enraged at Governor Denny for having passed the act and turned him out with threats of suing him for breach of instructions. But he had done it at the instance of the General, and for His Majesty's service, and having powerful interest at court, despised the threats and they were never put in execution.

[Here ends the autobiography]

Appendix A: Electrical Kite

To Peter Collinson, Oct. 19, 1752.

Sir,

As frequent mention is made in public papers from Europe of the success of the *Philadelphia* experiment for drawing electric fire from clouds by means of pointed rods of iron erected on high buildings, it may be agreeable to the curious to be informed that the same experiment has succeeded in *Philadelphia*, though made in a different and more easy manner, as follows:

Make a small cross of two light strips of cedar, the arms so long as to reach to the four corners of a large, thin silk handkerchief when extended. Tie the corners of the handkerchief to the extremities of the cross so you have the body of a kite, which being properly accommodated with a tail, loop, and string, will rise in the air, like those made of paper; but this being of silk, is fitter to bear the wet and wind of a thunder-gust without tearing.

To the top of the upright stick of the cross is to be fixed a very sharp-pointed wire, rising a foot or more above the wood. To the end of the twine, next to the hand, is to be tied a silk ribbon, and where the silk and twine join, a key may be fastened.

This kite is to be raised when a thunder-gust appears to be coming on, and the person who holds the string must stand under some cover so that the silk ribbon may not be wet; and care must be taken that the twine does not touch the frame of the door or window.

As soon as any of the thunder clouds come over the kite, the pointed wire will draw the electric fire from them, and the kite, with all the twine will be electrified, and the loose filaments of the twine will stand out every way and be attracted by an approaching finger.

When the rain has wet the kite and twine so that it can conduct the electric fire freely, you will find it stream out plentifully from the key on the approach of your knuckle. At this key the phial may be charged, and from electric fire thus obtained, spirits may be kindled, and all the electric experiments be performed, which are usually done by the help of a rubbed glass globe or tube, and thereby the sameness of the electric matter with that of lightning completely demonstrated.

B. Franklin

Appendix B: The Way to Wealth

From "Father Abraham's Speech," forming the preface to Poor *Richard's Almanac* for 1758.

It would be thought a hard Government that should tax its people one-tenth of their *Time*, to be employed in its Service. But *Idleness* taxes many of us much more, if we reckon all that is spent in absolute *Sloth*, or doing nothing, with that which is spent in idle employments or amusements that amount to nothing.

Sloth, by bringing on diseases, absolutely shortens Life. *Sloth, like rust, consumes faster than labor wears, while the used key is always bright, as Poor Richard says*

But dost thou love life, then do not squander time, for that's the stuff life is made of, as Poor Richard says. How much more than is necessary do we spend in sleep, forgetting that *the sleeping fox catches no poultry*, and that *there will be sleeping enough in the grave*, as *Poor Richard* says.

If time be of all things the most precious, wasting time must be, as Poor Richard says, *the greatest prodigality*; since, as he elsewhere tells us, *lost time is never found again, and what we call time enough, always proves little enough.* Let us then up and be doing, and doing to the purpose. So by diligence shall we do more with less perplexity.

Sloth makes all things difficult, but industry all easy, as *Poor Richard* says; and *He that riseth late must trot all day, and shall scarce overtake his business at night. Laziness travels so slowly, that Ppverty soon overtakes him*, as we read in *Poor Richard*, who adds, *Drive thy business, let not that drive thee*. And *early to bed, and early to rise, makes a man healthy, wealthy, and wise*.

Industry need not wish, and he that lives upon hope will die fasting.

There are no gains without pains.

He that hath a trade hath an estate, and he that hath a calling, hath an office of profit and honor. But then the *trade* must be worked at, and the *calling* well followed, or neither the *estate* nor the *office* will enable us to pay our taxes.

Though you have found no treasure, nor has any rich relation left you a legacy, *diligence is the mother of good-luck*, as *Poor Richard* says, *and God gives all things to industry*.

One today is worth two tomorrows, and farther, *have you somewhat to do tomorrow, do it today.*

If you were a servant, would you not be ashamed that a good master should catch you idle? Are you then your own master, *be ashamed to catch yourself idle*.

Stick to it steadily and you will see great effects, for *constant dropping wears away stones*, and by *diligence and patience the mouse ate in two the cable*; and *little strokes fell great oaks.*

Methinks I hear some of you say, *Must a man afford himself no leisure?* I will tell thee, my friend, what *Poor Richard* says, *Employ thy time well, if thou meanest to gain leisure, and since thou art not sure of a minute, throw not away an hour.*

Leisure is time for doing something useful. This leisure the diligent man will obtain, but the lazy man never. As *Poor Richard* says, *a life of leisure and a life of laziness are two things.*

Keep thy shop, and thy shop will keep thee. And, *If you would have your business done, go; if not, send.*

If you would have a faithful servant, and one that you like, serve yourself.

A little neglect may breed great mischief.

For want of a nail the shoe was lost; for want of a shoe the horse was lost; and for want of a horse the rider was lost, being overtaken and slain by the enemy; all for the want of care about a horse-shoe nail.

So much for industry and attention to one's own business. But to these we must add *frugality.*

What maintains one vice would bring up two Children. You may think perhaps, that a *little* tea, or a *little* punch now and then, diet a *little* more costly, clothes a *little* finer, and a *little* entertainment now and then, can be no *great* matter; but remember what *Poor Richard* says, *Many a little makes a mickle.*

Beware of little expenses: A small leak will sink a great ship. And, *who dainties love, shall beggars prove.* Moreover, *fools make feasts, and wise men eat them.*

Buy what thou hast no need of, and ere long thou shalt sell thy necessaries.

If you would know the value of money, go and try to borrow some, for he that goes a borrowing goes a sorrowing.

The second vice is lying, the first is running in debt. *Lying rides upon debt's back.*

Poverty often deprives a man of all spirit and virtue: *'Tis hard for an empty bag to stand upright.*

And now to conclude, *experience keeps a dear school, but fools will learn in no other, and scarce in that*; for it is true, *we may give advice, but we cannot give conduct.* However, remember this: *They that won't be counseled, can't be helped*, as *Poor Richard* says. And *if you will not hear Reason, she'll surely rap your knuckles.*

Appendix C: The Whistle

To Madame Brillon
Passy, November 10, 1779.

I am charmed with your description of paradise, and with your plan of living there, and I approve much of your conclusion that in the meantime we should draw all the good we can from this world. In my opinion, we might all draw more good from it than we do, and suffer less evil, if we would take care not to give too much for whistles. To me it seems that most of the unhappy people we meet with neglect that caution.

You ask what I mean? You love stories, and will excuse my telling one of myself.

When I was a child of seven year old, my friends, on a holiday, filled my pocket with coppers. I went directly to a shop where they sold toys for children. Being charmed with the sound of a *whistle* that I saw in the hands of another boy, I voluntarily offered and gave all my money for one. I came home and went whistling all over the house, much pleased with my *whistle*, but disturbing all the family.

My brothers, sisters, and cousins, understanding the bargain I had made, told me I had given four times as much as it was worth and put me in mind what good things I might have bought with the rest of the money, They laughed at me so much for my folly that I cried with vexation, and the reflection gave me more chagrin than the *whistle* gave me pleasure.

This was afterwards of use to me, for when I was tempted to buy some unnecessary thing, I often said to myself, *Don't give too much for the whistle*; and I saved my money.

As I grew up, came into the world, and observed the actions of men, I thought I met with many, very many, who *gave too much for the whistle.*

When I saw one too ambitious of court favor, sacrificing his time in attendance on levees, his repose, his liberty, his virtue, and perhaps his friends, to attain it, I have said to myself, *this man gives too much for his whistle.*

When I saw another fond of popularity, constantly employing himself in political bustles, neglecting his own affairs, and ruining them by neglect, *he pays, indeed*, said I, *too much for his whistle.*

If I knew a miser who gave up every kind of comfortable living, all the pleasure of doing good to others, all the esteem of his fellow citizens, and the joys of benevolent friendship, for the sake of accumulating wealth, *poor man*, said I, *you pay too much for your whistle.*

When I met with a man of pleasure, sacrificing every laudable improvement of the mind, or of his fortune, to mere corporeal sensations, and ruining his health in their pursuit, *mistaken man*, said I, *you are providing pain for yourself, instead of pleasure; you give too much for your whistle.*

If I see one fond of appearance, or fine clothes, fine houses, fine furniture, fine equipages, all above his fortune, for which he contracts debts, and ends his career in a prison, *alas!* say I, *he has paid dear, very dear, for his whistle.*

When I see a beautiful, sweet-tempered girl married to an ill-natured brute of a husband, *what a pity*, say I, *that she should pay so much for a whistle!*

In short, I conceive that the great part of the miseries brought upon mankind by the false estimates they have made of the value of things are by their *giving too much for their whistles.*

Yet I ought to have charity for these unhappy people when I consider that, with all this wisdom of which I am boasting, there are certain things in the world so tempting, for example, the apples of King John, which happily are not to be bought. For if they were put to sale by auction, I might very easily be led to ruin myself in the purchase, and find that I had once more given too much for the *whistle.*

Adieu, my dear friend, and believe me ever yours very sincerely and with unalterable affection,

B. Franklin

Appendix D: A Letter to Samuel Mather

Passy, May 12, 1784

Revd Sir,

It is now more than 60 years since I left Boston, but I remember well both your father and grandfather, having heard them both in the pulpit and seen them in their houses.

The last time I saw your father was in the beginning of 1724 when I visited him after my first trip to Pennsylvania. He received me in his library, and on my taking leave showed me a shorter way out of the house through a narrow passage which was crossed by a beam overhead.

We were still talking as I withdrew, he accompanying me behind, and I turning partly towards him, when he said hastily, "*Stoop, stoop!*" I did not understand him till I felt my head hit against the beam.

He was a man that never missed any occasion of giving instruction, and upon this he said to me, "*You are young, and have the world before you; stoop as you go through it, and you will miss many hard thumps.*" This advice, thus beat into my head, has frequently been of use to me. I often think of it when I see pride mortified and misfortunes brought upon people by their carrying their heads too high.

B. Franklin

Afterword: Abridging Ben

My abridgment of Franklin's autobiography brings me to offer the following observations:

- Although he worked at excellent composition and was considered a brilliant and entertaining writer, readers today will find his extensive use of semicolons, extremely long sentences, and interminable paragraphs rather inaccessible. I have replaced a large basketful of semicolons and comas with short sentences and periods.

- The first part of the book is easier to read, written to his son when Ben was a younger man. The last part, written when he was approaching age 80, if full of parliamentary rhetoric and required more effort on my part to make the paragraphs easily intelligible. My goal was for each sentence to make sense immediately. This required manipulation of his punctuation but not of his vocabulary, although I did omit some self-interrupting phrases that revealed little and obscured his meaning.

- The debate as to his religion comes clear very quickly. Raised in a strict Presbyterian home, he had Scripture ingrained in his psyche. His moral philosophy was shaped by biblical truth, but he himself seems to fit the description by the Apostle Paul of one who has a form of religion but denies its power. He clearly liked the practical value of virtue over vices in this life and may have presumed that good works stand for some value in the life to come.

- Having set out to shorten his 75,000 word document by half, I found the content of the first section pertaining to his youth to be fascinating with little room for abridgement. As my motive is to bring this story into the hands of university students, I left in almost everything having to do with his first 21 years, and especially of his extended "cross cultural" trip to England.

- The second section is of equal value for his contribution to good government, scientific innovation, and the establishment of a new nation. Here I was able to omit many needless words while laboring to retain the substance and style of his narrative.

- The claim that his is the best autobiography ever written may be plausible but would require a tremendous amount of reading to establish as fact. In all, I managed to erase 22,000 words which no one will miss but the meticulous reader of both documents.

- Not intended as a scholarly resource, this abridgment is meant for enjoyable and informative reading. Please use the original source (readily available online) for any direct quotes attributed to Franklin.

Daniel V. Runyon

Made in the USA
Middletown, DE
15 May 2016